Victoria College Belfast
The First 150 Years

Victoria College Belfast
The First 150 Years

JULIE KERR

BLACKSTAFF PRESS

Acknowledgements

Numerous people have helped with the compilation of *Victoria College Belfast: The First 150 Years*. I am grateful for the advice, assistance and expertise of the Anniversary Book Editorial Committee chaired so efficiently by Hilary Woods and composed of Joanne Brown, Professor David Hadden, Patricia Slevin, Mr John Wilson and Judy Young. Helen Wright, editor at Blackstaff Press, has been a tower of strength and has willingly put on many hats to help with the completion of this book. Janice Smith, copy-editor, worked long hours to accommodate our tight schedule. I thank Helen, Janice and the team at Blackstaff for their guidance, dedication and incredible patience. Jennie McCarter and Alison Wray sifted through and scanned numerous photographs and documents; Nicola Mawhinney, Ann Kirkpatrick and the school office staff readily assisted with providing information, documents and meeting rooms. Patricia Pyne's stunning photographs of the school and Drumglass House today greatly enhance the book.

The early chapters on Margaret Byers, the founder of Victoria College, draw on the meticulous research of Dr Alison Jordan, a former pupil of the school and member of the teaching staff, whose monograph, *Margaret Byers: Pioneer of Women's Education and Founder of Victoria College, Belfast*, was published in 1990, shortly before her premature death. The work of the 1959 Centenary Committee has been of immense help. Its members produced a book (*Victoria College Belfast Centenary 1859–1959*) celebrating the school's first hundred years and, crucially, interviewed and recorded the memories of Old Girls who had been pupils in Dr Byers' day. *Victoria College Belfast: The First 150 Years* relies extensively on the annual issues of *The Victorian* magazine, a valuable and inspiring record of school life, developments in education and the impact of national and international affairs. Thanks to everyone who has contributed to these magazines over the years.

This book seeks to chart the development of Victoria College as an institution and to place it within the context of educational, social and political change. But it aims also to open a window on to the daily life of the generations of pupils and staff who are the very heart of the school. I am indebted to all those who so kindly shared their memories, anecdotes and photographs and hope that their recollections will evoke a familiar past for former classmates and colleagues. I am particularly grateful to Ann Morrison and Patricia Pyne, former members of the teaching staff. My greatest thanks are to my mother, Betty Kerr, who for the last six months has faced a daily bombardment of telephone calls, requests and demands. Sleep has been disturbed, soup has gone cold and *Emmerdale* has been missed. Yet she has remained willing and good-humoured throughout, gladly sacrificing these pleasures for the school she so loves. Her help and interest have been a tremendous support.

pp. 2–3: Victoria College today; p. 6: garland swag leaded widow, Drumglass

First published in 2009 by
Blackstaff Press
4c Heron Wharf
Sydenham Business Park
Belfast BT3 9LE
and
Victoria College Belfast

Designed by Lisa Dynan
Printed by Nicholson & Bass, County Antrim

A CIP catalogue record for this book is available from the British Library

ISBN 978-0-85640-846-5

www.blackstaffpress.com
www.victoriacollege.org.uk

The history of this famous establishment is a veritable romance, a wonderful example of what can be accomplished by the genius, the industry and the personality of one woman.

NORTHERN WHIG, 25 JUNE 1914

Contents

A prophetic vision and the realisation of a dream

The Ladies' Collegiate School, Belfast

In 1853 Margaret Morrow Byers returned home to County Down from the mission field in China. She was just twenty years of age but already a mother and a widow. Margaret had left Ireland the previous year, shortly after her marriage to the Reverend John Byers, who had been commissioned by the Presbyterian Church to work as a missionary in Shanghai. Soon after their arrival in China he contracted a serious illness, and on medical advice the couple prepared to leave for the United States, hoping that John might be cured there. Margaret was at this time pregnant, and just before they were due to set sail she gave birth prematurely to their son, who was named after his father. The very next day they boarded the boat to America.

Unfortunately, the Reverend John Byers did not survive the journey. He died eight days before the boat reached New York and was buried in the city's Green-Wood Cemetery. Margaret made the arduous journey back to Ireland with her baby son. The future she had so eagerly anticipated a year before would never be realised. Yet Margaret Morrow Byers responded magnificently to her misfortune; she displayed the strength, determination and, critically, the faith that would make her the celebrated founder of Victoria College Belfast and her name synonymous with women's education and welfare work in Ireland.

Margaret Byers, *c.*1885

MARGARET MORROW

Mrs Byers had a dignified bearing, fine brown eyes, a sudden sunny smile
and beautiful white hands.

MELISSA HULL[1]

Margaret Morrow was born at Windsor Hill, Rathfriland, County Down, on 15 April 1832.
Her parents were Andrew Morrow, farmer and linen merchant, and Margaret (née Herron),
who was almost fifty at the time of her daughter's birth. The young Margaret experienced
loss at an early age for her father died when she was only eight. She was sent to Nottingham
to complete her education at Mrs Traffry's boarding school and later became a teacher there.
These years had a profound impact on her vision of education, for the headmistress of the
school promoted the cause of women teachers and impressed upon her pupils that women
could do anything under God. These were ideals that Margaret later upheld to advance
education in Ireland.

In February 1852 Margaret returned to Ireland to marry the Reverend John Byers;
after their wedding, the couple planned to serve in the mission field in China. The tragic and

premature death of her husband only a year later prompted Margaret to return to teaching, a decision that altered the course of her life and had a radical impact on the future of women's education.

Margaret had not initially intended to remain in Ireland and had been offered the job of establishing a mission school at Agra in India. But her mother persuaded her to stay and Margaret subsequently applied for the headship of the Ladies' Collegiate School, Cookstown, County Tyrone. She was chosen over 120 applicants but found her work there difficult since the local gentry and professional class were reluctant to send their daughters to school with the children of farmers and shopkeepers, and invariably employed governesses. It was thus difficult to sustain 'a well-equipped school in a country town'.[2] Margaret was advised and encouraged by friends to open her own school in Belfast, a town on the cusp of a radical and unprecedented expansion and, importantly, with a growing middle class whose daughters would need an education. Belfast was accorded city status in 1888, and between the 1860s and the end of the century its population tripled, making it the fastest growing industrial city in the British Isles.[3] Margaret Byers neither knew nor was known in Belfast, but the opportunities the city afforded persuaded her to relocate, and in the summer of 1859 she opened the Establishment for the Boarding and Education of Young Ladies. It was soon known affectionately as 'Mrs Byers' school'. The principal was only twenty-six years of age.

MRS BYERS' SCHOOL: AN EDUCATION FOR GIRLS

My aim is to provide for girls an education adapted to their wants as thorough as that which is afforded to boys in schools of the highest order; in fact, to work out a practical and well considered plan of education in which due regard should be given to the solid branches of learning as well as to a moral and religious training.
MARGARET BYERS[4]

Mrs Byers firmly believed that girls should receive a comprehensive education equal to that afforded to boys. Like Frances Buss and Dorothea Beale, the respective founders of the North London Collegiate School (1850) and Cheltenham Ladies' College (1853), she criticised the shallowness and superficiality of girls' education, which lacked solid learning and essentially taught them to paint, sing, play the piano and speak a little French. These pioneering women argued that girls should receive a rounded academic training, centred on arithmetic, English grammar, science and languages. Moreover, they believed that learning should begin early, ideally at four years of age, and continue through primary, secondary and even tertiary level. A solid education was essential to any girl who needed to earn a living and enter a respectable profession, and the self-supporting woman was very much a reality in the modern world.

It was with this vision that Margaret Byers opened her school at 13 Wellington Place on the corner of Queen Street. It was one of thirty-three girls' schools in Belfast, but it was well situated, since most of the middle class at this time lived in the centre of town. The school was also close to the Royal Belfast Academical Institution (RBAI) for boys at College Square East. The real key to its success, however, was its principal, whose determination and commitment

Mrs Byers (back row, seventh from left) with some senior pupils and her son, John Byers, *c*.1864

to provide a comprehensive education for girls ensured the school's survival.

As a newcomer to Belfast, Mrs Byers initially relied on a core of residential pupils; thirteen of the thirty-five pupils boarded. She offered the girls a solid education, teaching English grammar, arithmetic, Euclid (the Father of Geometry), modern history and natural science. This curriculum was quite different to that taught in other girls' schools, but it was clearly popular for Mrs Byers drew an ever-increasing number of pupils from Belfast, the surrounding countryside and farther afield. Larger premises were soon needed and the school relocated to 10 Howard Street, but the pressure of numbers forced a second move. Mrs Byers was unable to find premises to meet her needs and therefore decided to build a double-fronted house on the Dublin Road at 74–76 Pakenham Place. Number 74 served as her private residence, while the classrooms and bedrooms for the boarders were located in the adjoining house. In 1867 the new school was opened and renamed the Ladies' Collegiate School, Belfast.

At this time, sixty of the girls boarded or stayed with friends in the town, while the remainder were from local families. The school day began at 9 a.m. with prayers led by the principal. Lessons followed, and in the afternoon the boarders would go for their daily walk up the Malone, Stranmillis or Lisburn roads. With the roomier premises at Pakenham Place, a wider range of subjects could be taught, and the girls participated in dancing and needlework. Mrs Byers saw the provision of such activities as essential; she insisted that womanly skills, physical health and a moral character should be nurtured alongside the intellect; education ought to encompass a breadth of learning and experiences.

Within ten years of her arrival in Belfast, Mrs Byers had established a successful school and attracted a wide circle of friends and supporters. Pupils were drawn from all over Ireland and numbers were rising rapidly. This had been achieved without any financial assistance. It had been, and remained, Mrs Byers' private venture and the success or failure of the school rested on her shoulders. Margaret Byers was not simply a committed educationalist, but a shrewd businesswoman and an entrepreneur.

LOWER CRESCENT: THE REALISATION OF A DREAM

The college was then city-bound, though as always, ruralised by its setting, the great airy building so imaginatively planned by her in 1874, its noble façade on the Crescent, with casements opening on the grass courts, more adapted to the cultivation of friendship than of tennis.

E. MAUD FARRINGTON (NÉE WHITE)[5]

The school at Pakenham Place flourished and was testimony to the success and passion of its founder. However, growing numbers meant that the building no longer adequately accommodated the pupils. Nor could it provide the facilities that Mrs Byers considered essential to a comprehensive education. While it was customary for girls to be educated in small schools – many feared that large institutions would be damaging to the girls' morals and manners – Mrs Byers insisted that girls could only progress if they, like boys, were taught in large schools. More pupils on the register would mean that schools could be better equipped, a greater number of teachers employed and a wider range of subjects offered. Furthermore, classes could then be divided and subdivided according to ability, so that each girl could be given the time and attention she required.

Undeterred by public opinion and undaunted by the costs involved, Mrs Byers proceeded to realise her vision and planned the first purpose-built girls' school. This was a huge challenge and a massive financial undertaking, since the school was Mrs Byers' private enterprise and she herself was liable for the loan and any problems that arose. A site was duly acquired at Lower Crescent, south Belfast, and the architects, Young and Mackenzie, were engaged to design a building tailor-made to suit the needs of the Ladies' Collegiate. Mrs Byers borrowed £7,000 for the building work; with interest rates charged at 5 per cent per annum, plus ground rent and taxes, she would be required to pay back the considerable yearly sum of £500. Yet she proceeded with conviction, determined to prove that a college such as hers could be made a commercial success out of its own earnings 'with a little economy' and sound management.[6] Work on the new school began in the autumn of 1873, and on 27 August 1874 the building was formally opened by Mrs William Grey, founder of the Women's Education Movement. There were over two hundred girls on the register.

The new school was built of Scrabo stone and arranged over four floors. It was entered via large double doors on Lower Crescent. Mrs Byers' private residence adjoined the school, but its entrance was on University Road and her rooms were strictly out of bounds. As one former pupil recalled, the principal's quarters were separated from the classrooms by a heavily curtained door, beyond which 'lay a very deeply respected, even awesome unknown'.[7] The school was well equipped and had its own lecture hall, where the girls met each morning for assembly, sat examinations and gathered for the annual prize distribution. There were classrooms, music rooms and a state-of-the-art gymnasium, which was the first of its kind in Ireland. Mrs Byers regarded exercise essential to the girls' daily regime and was extremely proud of the school's gymnasium. The bedrooms and bathrooms for the boarders and resident staff were on the second and third floors, while their dining room was on the ground floor. Cooked meals were not served to day girls, who generally brought a mid-morning snack of bread and jam from home. The health of the pupils was always an important consideration and the new school had its own sanatorium, which was run by Mrs Byers' son, John (later Sir John Byers), a former pupil of RBAI and a distinguished doctor (see page 19).

A SYSTEMATIC EDUCATION

I look back to that remote autumn day when I first stood on the
steps of Victoria College, my heart fluttering [...] I can still recall the
chill of my entry into the august reception room, dominated by
the larger-than-human portrait of the founder, stately and commanding.
What a relief it was after some agonising moments to be confronted
with her in person, less picturesque in contemporary garb but with
undiminished dignity and the same benign and sensitive face.
E. MAUD FARRINGTON (NÉE WHITE) [8]

The school at Lower Crescent was a source of great pride to Mrs Byers. For the first time girls had the opportunity to receive a solid and systematic education equal to that available to boys. Learning began early. Four-year-olds – both boys and girls – were admitted to the preparatory department at kindergarten level, where they were taught according to the newly launched Froebel system. This sought to stimulate learning through group games and individual play. The children enjoyed activities such as modelling in clay and sand, basket-weaving and caring for animals 'as far as is possible'.[9] At eight years of age, the boys left the school. Girls continued in the preparatory department until they were eleven, but their curriculum was expanded. In addition to basic subjects such as reading, writing and geography, they now learned arithmetic, grammar, British history and needlework.

Eleven-year-olds who had completed their education in the preparatory classes progressed to the intermediate department, but newcomers had first to pass an entrance examination set by the school. The syllabus was extended at each level of learning, and girls in the intermediate department were introduced to an array of new subjects including ancient

The Lower Crescent school, *c*.1908

The examination hall, *c.*1908

history, map-drawing, Latin and modern languages. Class tests were held three times a year and were valued as a way to assess pupils, but they were also intended to instil discipline and provide an aid to learning. In addition, girls in the intermediate department were encouraged, but not compelled, to take the London Royal College of Preceptors examinations. These were not widely recognised, but it was hoped that the Royal Commission on Endowed Schools, which had been formed in 1858, would introduce changes and enable girls, like boys, to sit accredited public examinations.

At fifteen years of age the intermediate girls took an admission test for the advanced department. This part of the school comprised a junior and a senior collegiate, and sound teaching was guaranteed. Pupils were introduced to new subjects, which included English literature, geometry and algebra, as well as logic, political economy and bookkeeping. From 1870 girls in the senior collegiate had the opportunity to sit public examinations set by the Queen's University of Ireland (QUI), which awarded certificates to successful candidates. Those wishing to train as teachers also attended the senior collegiate classes; these students only had to pay half the usual tuition fees.

Sir John Byers and his son

Health

The health of the girls was a primary concern for Mrs Byers, and when the new school opened at Lower Crescent in 1874, she made sure it had its own sanatorium. This was run by Mrs Byers' son, John, who was later knighted for his services as professor of midwifery and the diseases of women and children at the Queen's College, Belfast. John Byers also had consulting rooms at Lower Crescent and was closely involved in the running of the school, even after his mother's death in 1912.

The sanatorium adjoined the main building but was accessed from the side of the house so that the girls could be isolated, for example, in the case of an epidemic. Such an epidemic could have serious consequences and even force the school to close. Indeed, literally months after the opening of the Lower Crescent school, there was an outbreak of scarlet fever in the boarding department. A number of parents thought the school should shut to prevent the infection spreading but, fortunately, the Reverend Dr Watts of the Presbyterian Assembly College, a parent and a firm supporter of its principal, came to the rescue. He offered Mrs Byers the use of classrooms at the Assembly College so that the day girls could continue their studies uninterrupted. The infected pupils were transferred to a private ward at the Belfast Royal Hospital and it was planned to close the boarding department for four months. Eighteen

of the resident pupils feared that the temporary closure of the boarding department would be injurious to the school's future, for other girls might be reluctant to return. Accordingly they pledged to stay in the boarding department and continue their lessons in quarantine. For seven weeks these brave girls remained in the school and were taught by a few of the resident staff. Mrs Byers was overwhelmed by their courage and loyalty. In her annual report she paid tribute to their self-sacrifice, which, she claimed, had undoubtedly secured the prosperity of the school.[10]

The Ladies' Collegiate survived the epidemic, but Mrs Byers was eager to reassure parents that their daughters' health remained a primary concern. Each year she would invariably begin her report with a comment on the girls' health, which was generally good. Occasionally she had to report the death of a pupil. One particularly poignant memorial appears in the school magazine for 1889. It is a poem written by Mrs Byers to comfort one of her pupils, Maggie, who had recently lost her sister, Minnie. The final verse reads:

> When you grieve and wish for Minnie
> She's not lost but gone before
> Think of that and follow after
> Christ's the way, the open Door[11]

Some years later, in October 1918, when Miss Matier was principal of Victoria College, there was a severe outbreak of influenza in Belfast. The school did not escape unscathed and the sanatorium was soon full of pupils and members of the teaching staff. It was decided that all boarders who were well enough to travel should return home and that the school should close until the sickness abated. Laura Patterson (née Wood), a pupil at the time, lived in Galway, and since the journey was too long for her to make on her own, she remained at the school with several of the elderly mistresses. When they too became ill, she was sent to Bangor with Mademoiselle Oppliger, the resident French mistress and acting assistant matron. For two weeks the pair took walks along the shore and Mademoiselle Oppliger taught Laura 'the German or Swiss' way to knit.[12]

A BREADTH OF LEARNING

The girls of the Ladies' Collegiate enjoyed the fullest kind of education and were encouraged to develop every faculty 'in a free and healthy activity'.[13] Physical exercise was considered an integral part of the school day, particularly as the girls were city-bound and had a relatively sedentary lifestyle. They played outdoor sports such as tennis and hockey, and took swimming lessons; according to one former pupil, Mrs Byers had hoped to build the school its own swimming pool, something that was quite unprecedented at this time.[14] Dancing and exercise classes were conducted in the new gymnasium. The format of these classes was shaped by current fashions but effectively consisted of drill exercises and dancing with hoops and tambourines. Calisthenics was popular in the early days, while 'the physical exercises of Dr Roth, who has given many years' study to hygienic reform' were introduced later.[15] Not every girl shared her principal's enthusiasm for exercise, and on several occasions Mrs Byers noted that the gymnasium was not used as much as she would wish and urged parents to be less quick to provide their daughters with excuse notes.[16]

While the girls were to strive for academic excellence, they were not to ignore the skills necessary for homemakers. When the school relocated to Lower Crescent, a 'chef de cuisine' was brought in to teach cookery; the girls learned how to prepare and truss fowl for roasting and boiling, make the perfect soufflé and cook curry. There were needlework classes and from 1879 a gold and a silver thimble were awarded annually to the two girls who could hem, fell and top-seam 'with as much dexterity as when the term "Higher Education" was unknown'.[17] Mrs Byers sought to provide her girls with every possible opportunity and took full advantage of Belfast's talents. Following the establishment of the School of Art in 1870, she arranged for the masters there to set up a drawing department in the Ladies' Collegiate. The classes were so

The tennis courts at the
Lower Crescent school, c.1908

popular that a sketching club was formed. The organist of Fisherwick Church offered tuition in choral music, and the girls were able to take private piano and violin lessons. The resident pupils could learn to ride.[18]

While the girls at the Ladies' Collegiate learned a wide range of subjects and acquired a variety of skills, they were reminded that their conduct in life would be the real test of the education they received at school. Ultimately the purpose of education was to form character.[19]

Excerpts from 'Our College'

Ah! No, thy mission has a wider field,
Than that which book or dry routine can yield;
Thy chief endeavour is, with perfect art
(And surely 'tis the nobler, better part)
To train the mind and cultivate the heart.

Gymnastics fill the hoyden heart with glee
And slöjd gives scope to neat dexterity;
refining Art has charms for sweet sixteen
although the needful, yet despised routine
excites betimes the youthful artist's spleen.

From tiny rooms just off the corridor
issue sweet strains of Mendelssohn and Spohr,
now plaintive minor scales ring out so clear
or Czerny's exercise greet the ear –
sad fruit of aching heart and bitter tear!

'NORA'[20]

THE SCHOOL DAY

Oh what bliss it was to be alive! Victoria was the best school in Ulster.
Mrs Byers, the Head, was a wonderful old lady who made a grand
tour of the classrooms every day; all the girls rose to their feet at her
entrance and remained respectfully standing until her exit.
CATHLEEN NESBITT[21]

The school year was divided into four terms with a two-week break at Christmas and an eight-week holiday that commenced in midsummer. The school day began with assembly in the lecture hall at 9 a.m. This was led by Mrs Byers, who read a passage from the Bible 'with vim and vigour'. She remained seated on the dais while the girls took their morning constitutional – a bracing march around the room to music. Each girl bowed to the principal before she left the hall and, as one former pupil explained, the 'charming smile' they received inspired them for the day's work.[22] Mrs Byers retained an active interest in every aspect of the Ladies' Collegiate and was a visible presence in the school. She visited each class to take the daily roll

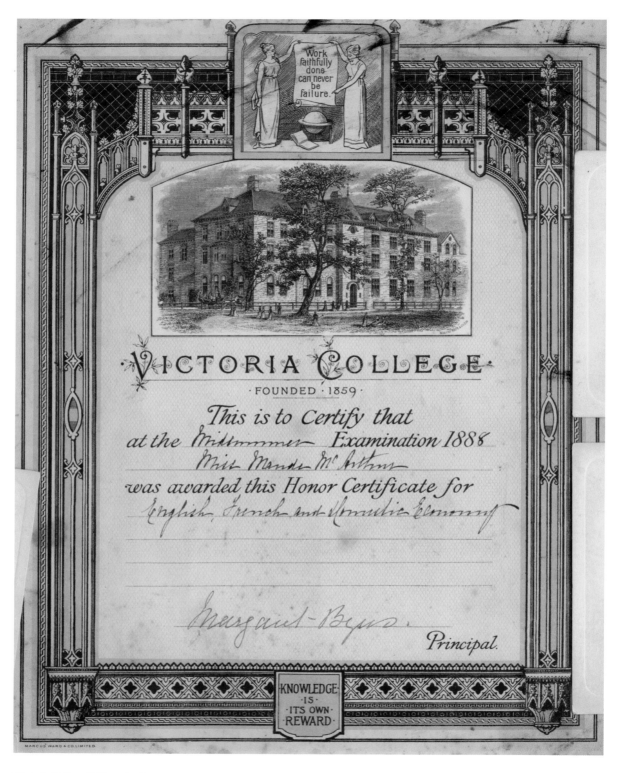

Victoria College Belfast school
examination certificate, 1888

call and would invariably correct any slackness, enquire about the girls' health or ask after their parents.[23] Lessons ran from 9.30 a.m. until 2.30 p.m., with a short break at 11 a.m. when pupils ate a snack. The preparatory department began at 10 a.m. and the youngest children went home at 1 p.m.

After school the girls had time for recreation, although they were also expected to prepare for the following day's classes. Mrs Byers urged parents to support their daughters' learning by providing them with a quiet place to study in the evening, away from the family circle; she recommended two hours of study a night and reassured parents that this was not excessive and would have no ill affects on their daughters' health. Otherwise, the girls were free to enjoy their leisure time. The boarders had an afternoon walk two-by-two – the renowned 'croc' – and they would then dance or play the piano. The day girls had greater freedom and often met in the Botanical Gardens; in better weather they bathed at the seaside. Mrs Byers was insistent that even out of school her girls should act with decorum and she was known to complain about 'bits of boys and chits of girls gadding about together'.[24] Still, there was opportunity for the two to mix. Mrs Byers would host 'at homes', to which the boarders invited their brothers from RBAI for tea and parlour games; they in turn were asked to take tea with the principal of RBAI and were invariably invited to celebratory dances commemorating the boys' sporting victories.[25]

The day girls and boarders seldom mixed after school, but they did come together at school societies such as the Crescent Literary Society, which was formed during the academic year of 1876–7 and revived in 1886. This was intended for senior girls who were over eighteen. They met 'on equal terms' to cultivate their thoughts and improve their eloquence. The society met in Mrs Byers' drawing room and heard papers given by visiting speakers and members of staff. The topics were wide ranging and included 'public opinion', 'medical training for women' and 'whether the stage should be abolished'. Former students and outsiders were invited to join the group and considered it a great honour to be included in these erudite discussions. It was important that members contributed to these discussions, but, as Mrs Byers warned, talking was like playing the harp and there was a time for silence – 'there is as much in laying the hands on the strings to stop their vibrations as in twanging them to bring out their music'.[26]

A VISION OF LEARNING:
MRS BYERS, PUBLIC EXAMINATIONS
AND A GROWING CURRICULUM

Mrs Byers led the way in Belfast entering girls for public examinations,
using progressive teaching techniques, encouraging her girls to
become teachers and missionaries at a time when women were often
encouraged to stay at home; and in running a business.
ALISON JORDAN[27]

This was a formative time for education in Ireland and Margaret Byers played a pivotal role in securing advances for women, particularly their right to sit public examinations and to take their place in the teaching profession. When Mrs Byers arrived in Belfast in 1859, there were hopes for great changes in education, for a Royal Commission on Endowed Schools had been set up the previous year to consider the introduction of a state-supported system of intermediate education. Progress was slow, but in 1878 the results of the enquiry led to the proposal of an Intermediate Education Bill for Ireland. The Bill proposed to set up an Intermediate Board of Education that would be responsible for organising public examinations and maintaining standards in the schools – 'a kind of Victorian Education and Library Board'.[28] Schools and individual pupils would be rewarded for their achievements with 'result fees' paid to school managers for pupil passes and prizes awarded to top students. The initiative was to be funded by a £1m endowment resulting from the disestablishment of the Church of Ireland in 1871; this sum would be supplemented by revenue from the Customs and Excise grant known as the Whiskey Fund.

While educational reformists such as Margaret Byers supported the proposals, they were shocked that the Bill as it stood applied only to boys and duly mounted a campaign for its modification. Mrs Byers and her friend, Miss Isabella Tod, the leading activist in women's rights in Ireland, headed a deputation that travelled to London to petition Lord Chancellor Cairns. Mrs Byers later recalled that while Lord Chancellor Cairns was a Belfast man, he was unfamiliar with recent educational developments in Ireland. On learning that senior girls had been sitting public examinations run by the QUI since 1870 and had achieved remarkable success, he was delighted and surprised. Most of the candidates whose results had been quoted to the Lord Chancellor were Mrs Byers' pupils, and their achievement convinced him to extend the Bill to girls. The Intermediate Education Act 1878 revolutionised education in Ireland. For the first time girls had the same opportunity as boys to sit accredited public examinations, granting them a platform on which to demonstrate their academic abilities.

Mrs Byers responded immediately to the new developments and put her school on an examination footing. In January 1879 the girls of the Ladies' Collegiate were entered into the first Intermediate examinations, to be held that June. They did remarkably well and subsequently dominated the top of the results' table, carrying off the majority of the prizes. In 1889 the Ladies' Collegiate attained forty-eight distinctions, while its nearest rival, Alexandra College, Dublin, secured twenty-three. In Belfast, Methodist College obtained eleven and Princess Gardens two. However, there was not universal praise for the girls' 'phenomenal success'. In September 1892 the *Dublin Evening Mail* referred to 'a nefarious non-Catholic girls' school in Belfast that simply grabs nearly all the prizes' and declared that the separate girls' department of the Intermediate Board seemed to exist 'especially for this college'.[29] But generally the girls' achievements were celebrated and the publication of their examination results brought honour to the school. Moreover, the fact that the pupils of the Ladies' Collegiate, taught by female teachers, outperformed girls in mixed schools who were taught by men, was clear proof of women's abilities as teachers and a justification of their place in the profession.[30]

Mrs Byers took great pleasure in the school's success. Each year she cut out the lists of examination results from the newspapers and carefully pasted them into her scrapbooks, along with any other noteworthy reports on educational reform. On prize days she would recount the girls' results with great pride and emotion, and pay tribute to their achievements. Mrs Byers

firmly believed that the key to their success was a systematic education and urged parents to start their daughters' education at an early age. While good results in the examination hall were important, Mrs Byers reminded her pupils that the victories won in a hundred examinations could not compensate for 'want of high moral tone, one grace of the spirit or one womanly excellence'.[31] Indeed, she maintained that the school's greatest success could not be tested by examinations. It lay instead in the careful supervision and individualisation of teaching that each pupil received. Regardless of her ability or disposition, every girl at the Ladies' Collegiate was helped to realise her potential and 'fill the niche in life possible to each'.[32]

RESTRUCTURING THE SCHOOL

The education reforms introduced by the Intermediate Education Act 1878 meant that structural changes at the school were needed together with modifications to the curriculum. Pupils now entered the intermediate department when they were ten years of age and remained until eighteen. The classes prepared them for the Intermediate Board examinations, although not every pupil took these. Some opted out as they or their parents considered examinations overly stressful. Others were not entered since they had not reached the required standard. These were generally girls who had started their education late, leaving their teachers too little time to prepare them for the examinations; as Mrs Byers colourfully explained, it would be like trying to pour a pint of milk into a quart container.[33] Whether or not the girls sat the examinations, they benefited from the studious atmosphere of the classroom. The revised curriculum comprised English, mathematics, natural science and scripture. Both English and mathematics were umbrella terms – English consisted of spelling and reading, grammar and analysis, geography, history, map-drawing, theory of music, English language and literature, and composition; arithmetic, Euclid, algebra, bookkeeping, trigonometry and mechanics came under mathematics.

Structural changes in the advanced department followed shortly thereafter, a consequence of the formation of the Royal University Ireland (RUI) in 1880 and the decision to confer degrees on women. Margaret Byers responded by establishing her own collegiate department for her 'sweet girl graduates'.[34]

TERTIARY EDUCATION: 'THE JEWEL IN THE CROWN'[35]

In the seclusion of the most remote section of this frontage beyond the
pillars flourished the University House, a world apart, from which issued
every year a group of graduates, chiefly of the extern Royal University.
E. MAUD FARRINGTON (NÉE WHITE)[36]

From 1870 senior girls were able to sit public examinations set by the QUI, which had colleges in Belfast, Galway and Cork. This development owed much to the energy and determination of Margaret Byers, Miss Isabella Tod and the Ladies' Institute Belfast.[37] However, the arrangement was not wholly satisfactory since the QUI awarded certificates to the girls, not degrees. This changed in 1880 when Benjamin Disraeli's government replaced the QUI with the RUI, which had its headquarters in Dublin. The RUI was purely an examining board and conferred degrees on candidates regardless of their institution and irrespective of their sex. For the first time girls had the opportunity to obtain degrees and, accordingly, to compete with men in the workplace.

Mrs Byers was quick to respond. In 1881 she opened a collegiate department to prepare girls over eighteen for degrees awarded by the newly established RUI, as well as for Cambridge Higher local examinations. She rented 3 Lower Crescent, known as University House, where the girls were taught by a separate staff of certified lecturers from Ireland, the UK and Europe, and could sit honours and pass degrees, as well as MAs, in mathematics, mental and moral science, civil and constitutional history, political economy, general jurisprudence, Classics and modern literature.[38] The collegiate department was truly 'the jewel in the crown' of the Ladies' Collegiate School and a source of tremendous delight to the principal.[39] Indeed, Mrs Byers' was the only girls' school in Ulster, and one of only two in Ireland, to have both a high school and a collegiate department.

The Ladies' Collegiate invariably came top of all the girls' colleges in Ireland in the RUI examinations and took third place overall, behind the Queen's College, Belfast and University College Dublin. From 1891 to 1900, 95 of the 155 female graduates in Ireland were Mrs Byers' girls – a tremendous accolade.[40] A notable graduate of the collegiate department was Anne Acheson CBE (1882–1962), a celebrated sculptor and the first woman to be made a fellow of the Royal Society of British Sculptors. Anne graduated from the collegiate department in modern languages and taught briefly at the school before proceeding to the Royal College of Art.

The collegiate department was not just for those wishing to take degree examinations. Any girl over eighteen years of age who wanted to improve her knowledge of literature and science could attend the classes and indeed was greatly encouraged by Mrs Byers, who was emphatic that education should be ongoing. The collegiate department continued until 1908 when the Irish Universities Act replaced the RUI with the National University of Dublin, which had colleges in Cork and Galway and an independent university in Belfast – Queen's University Belfast. This development forced the closure of women's colleges, for while the RUI had conferred its degrees on candidates regardless of their institution, now only those who attended lectures at the university could sit the examinations. Thus if girls wished to obtain degrees, they had to enrol at Queen's. Mrs Byers opposed the new arrangements for she feared girls would be lost in the mixed environment of the university and was concerned that women would no longer have an opportunity to teach at tertiary level.[41] The loss of the 'jewel in the crown' was a tremendous blow, but Mrs Byers retained an active interest in higher education and in 1908 was invited to sit on the first senate of Queen's. Moreover, she provided the university with one of its most distinguished scholars, the writer, translator and medievalist Helen Waddell, who had attended Victoria College from 1901 to 1907 and graduated with a First Class Honours degree from Queen's in 1911.

'A STORM OF RIDICULE'[42]

'If study slays its tens, idleness and frivolity slay thousands.'
QUOTED BY MARGARET BYERS

At the school's annual prize distribution in 1887 Mrs Byers noted with pleasure the remarkable progress that had been made in girls' education over the previous thirty years. Girls could now receive a solid and systematic education, sit public examinations and obtain degrees; high achievers could be educated without costing their parents a penny. As she later remarked, 'a more congenial study is now generally substituted for the hopeless everlasting drill of unmusical girls at the piano'.[43] It had not been easy to secure these advances. Mrs Byers explained that they had had to overcome 'a storm of ridicule', for there were many who believed girls should be cosseted and deemed them unsuited to a proper education, which might be injurious to their health; furthermore, they feared that learning would stifle the girls' womanly qualities. Margaret Byers was quick to answer her critics and recommended that they direct their concerns to the girls in the workhouse. She pointed out that knowledge of Euclid hardly 'unfit its possessor for the handicraft of cookery or for mending a stocking with neatness and despatch'. She herself believed that domestic skills should be nurtured as part of a comprehensive education to supplement learning, and maintained that those who were diligent in the classroom would more likely be diligent in the home. Mrs Byers recounted the 'zest' with which some of the cleverest girls in her school 'entered into the mysteries' of everyday operations such as roasting and boiling, and hoped this would allay the terror that a wider education would distract women from their domestic duties. But the greatest proof, as she wryly noted, was that 'man's reverence for womanliness and woman's admiration of true manliness' had not been diminished by this 'comparative test of intellectual powers'.[44]

'The crown before us'

The Victoria College and School, Belfast

Altered thou art in name; in former days
'Collegiate School' in golden letters met our gaze
But now by edict of our gracious Queen
Inscribed upon thy portals may be seen
'Victoria College' more appropriate ween.

'NORA'[1]

The original brass nameplate of
Victoria College from Lower Crescent

In the summer of 1887 Queen Victoria conceded that in this, her jubilee year, the Ladies' Collegiate School, Belfast should be renamed the Victoria College and School, Belfast. The preparatory department would be known as the Victoria School, while the intermediate and collegiate departments would be called the Victoria College. Shortly thereafter the whole institution was known simply as Victoria College. The renaming of the school was a great honour and one that had been earned through academic excellence for, as Mrs Byers explained:

> We did not seek to change our name from the Ladies' Collegiate School
> to Victoria College until we had won our way by the establishment of
> classes for the different years in the Royal University course.[2]

The renaming of the school by royal command called for celebration, although some confessed that they felt 'a lingering love' for the old name and a sense of loss. One former pupil decided that positive action was better than 'maudlin sympathy'. She donated a sum of money to the scholarship committee and asked that it be called the Ladies' Collegiate School Prize, as a tribute to 'the old place' which she and her fellow classmates had considered 'a real alma mater'. This prize was to be awarded annually to a girl over eighteen years of age who could not afford to finance a university education.[3]

1887 brought other changes to the school, notably to its organisation. Growing numbers meant that extra classroom space was needed if classes were to be kept small. It was thus decided that the kindergarten and preparatory department should be relocated to the hall of the Crescent Church, and that the Lower Crescent building be reserved for the intermediate and collegiate departments. It was with great reluctance that Mrs Byers moved the younger children out of Lower Crescent, for she considered their presence a great asset to the school and would visit them regularly to lift her spirits. Now, as she explained, one had to cross the road, go through the tennis ground and climb a windy staircase before standing in front of 'a happy group of children'. Mrs Byers confessed that on the day of the transfer she had to fight back 'blinding tears' as she 'tried' to welcome the younger pupils to their new premises.[4]

THE STAFF AND DISCIPLINE

To a staff list of able women graduates, drawn from Dublin, Belfast,
Girton and Paris, the early records add the names of no fewer than nine
outstanding men, one of them a noted musician who, anticipating educational
theory by half a century, initiated choral singing and music appreciation.
D. FELICITAS CORRIGAN[5]

Victoria College was run as Mrs Byers' private enterprise, which meant she had sole responsibility for choosing her staff and deciding the pupil–teacher ratio. She believed that the standard of education rested firmly on the quality of the teachers. This meant that the school initially relied on students and professors from the Queen's College, Belfast. However, advances in tertiary education, beginning with the QUI's decision in 1870 to award women certificates and culminating in the conferment of degrees by the RUI ten years later, meant

Mrs Byers (centre) and her staff at Lower Crescent,
c.1879; Miss Matier is second on the left

that Mrs Byers could build up a predominantly female, highly qualified teaching staff and fulfil
her ambition of promoting women in the profession. Although men were always represented
on the staff of Victoria, she felt strongly that girls' schools should give preference to female
teachers since they had little chance of securing posts in either boys' schools or universities;
their only chance of a career was in teaching their own sex. Mrs Byers confessed she was
'quietly determined' to create an efficient staff of teachers from among her own pupils,
but she was open-minded and welcomed others who deserved an opportunity. Sister Mary
Gertrude of Loretto Abbey recalled how one of her own pupils had been engaged by Mrs
Byers as intermediate superintendent at Victoria College, since at that time only Protestant
establishments had university departments.[6]

To provide the highest standard of teaching and enthuse the girls, Mrs Byers' staff
taught by subject rather than class. Former pupils paid tribute to the calibre of teaching they
received and the strong work ethos in the school. Melissa Hull, a graduate of the collegiate
department, explained that Mrs Byers engaged the best teachers to provide 'excellent all-
round tuition' that was unparalleled anywhere else; she confessed that while they had not been
aware of this as girls, she was now greatly appreciative. Melissa became professor of English
at the University of Rio de Janeiro. She was awarded the OBE for her service to Brazil, and
shortly before her death in 1970, a lecture room in the English faculty at Niteroi was named

after her. Another former pupil recalled how much she had enjoyed her schooldays during which the teachers had inspired 'a taste for good literature'.[7]

The memories of past pupils reveal a tremendous fondness for their teachers, many of whom were strong and colourful characters who left a vivid impression on their students in what was clearly a vibrant institution. They evoke the homesick Fräulein, the 'bustling mademoiselle' and the young, male Classics teacher scared off by a class of fifteen-year-old girls; the organist of Fisherwick Church, who raised his baton over a mass of singers in the lecture hall, and the teacher they nicknamed Snake, since she fired out 'next, next' in a thick country accent.[8] In addition to the regular staff, several of whom were resident, Mrs Byers brought in outsiders to offer expert instruction. According to the school prospectus of 1889, 'a lady' taught 'plain and fancy needlework' and the master of the Belfast School of Art and his assistants offered instruction in painting and drawing, while Sergeant Whelan put the girls through their paces with musical drill and gymnastics.

> The teachers seemed to me splendid women with a real vocation, and the
> acquiring of knowledge became really exciting. I, who had always loathed
> arithmetic, fell in love with the mathematics teacher who had rabbit teeth
> sticking out oddly but even those seemed beautiful to me, and to gain merit
> in her eyes I applied myself eagerly to the magical world of mathematics.
> I was thrilled with algebra and Euclid and came to derive great pleasure in
> solving difficult problems. I even found them a game more fun than chess and
> one could play it alone. But the most exciting class was that of Miss MacWhirter,
> who taught history and literature and like Miss Jean Brodie she had her little
> group of special girls of whom Helen Waddell was the bright star, and to which
> I was admitted.
> CATHLEEN NESBITT[9]

Mrs Byers and her staff ran a tight ship. They were stern, if compelling, and inspired respect. Discipline was rarely a problem, but inevitably there were bouts of mischief. Miscreants were sent to the principal's office and whatever transpired there behind the closed door clearly had the desired effect:

> After this experience any suggestion of a repeated visit to the office was enough
> to strike terror and reduce the pupil to repentance and even to tears and
> promises of improvement.[10]

The girls were expected to act impeccably in public and the school had a reputation for good behaviour. There were occasional irregularities, such as the disruption three Victoria girls caused on a train in 1911. Mrs Margaret Morgan reported the incident to Miss Matier, the vice principal and acting head. She complained that the miscreants had changed carriages at every stop, stuck their heads out of the windows to shout at boys and, worse, had chanted at her 'Molly O'Morgan with her little organ'. The girls were no doubt severely reprimanded by Miss Matier, who was well known and widely feared for her caustic tongue that 'dragooned' the girls into good manners.[11]

Each term the girls' parents were sent an update on their progress, that reported on both academic work and conduct, noting any misdemeanours that had been committed.

DEVELOPMENTS AND CHANGES: THE CURRICULUM, FACILITIES AND EXTRACURRICULAR ACTIVITIES

The school was continually evolving, not only to meet the demands of educational reforms, but also because Mrs Byers was always seeking ways to improve the curriculum and exploit whatever new talents and opportunities became available. In addition, she kept abreast of developments in Great Britain, and each year, on her way to holiday with a friend in the south of England, she would break her journey in London to take a 'helpful peep' at the educational work in some of the schools and institutions there. Mrs Byers found these visits stimulating and insightful, and she remarked on one particularly well-organised school, run by a Miss Lord, whom she described as 'abreast if not in advance of most modern educational improvements'. Miss Lord had travelled widely on the Continent and introduced ideas and devices she had observed there to develop the pupils' minds and bodies. Some of these were adopted by Mrs Byers, who was clearly inspired by her visits to the school and felt an affinity with Miss Lord. She was greatly impressed by the elocution lessons that Miss Lord had introduced and was eager that her own girls should learn how to express themselves effectively in later life. Thus in September 1901 the 'much-sought after Miss Fogerty of London' arrived in Belfast to run a month-long elocution course at Victoria College; it was later deemed a tremendous success.[12]

Indeed, the range of subjects on the school curriculum was constantly growing in order to embrace new methods of teaching and to cultivate technical skills as much as intellectual prowess. A striking example of this is educational *slöjd*, a Swedish form of carving in soft wood which was intended to teach the importance of manual work, develop dexterity and creativity, and exercise muscles seldom used. Not least, it would improve pupils' ability to receive instruction. This was extremely popular in the late nineteenth century and was advocated by both Mrs Byers and Miss Lord. Mademoiselle Strömsten, who taught *slöjd* at Victoria College, translated the leading book on the subject from Swedish into English. Her endeavours merited a write-up in the local press: the *News Letter* hailed her translation 'a substantial contribution to educational science' and heartily recommended it to parents and educationalists so that they might understand the harmonious development of the body and the mind that resulted from the study of *slöjd*.[13] Miss Sarah Garrett also taught *slöjd* in addition to English, mathematics and natural philosophy. She wrote a lengthy article for the school magazine explaining its merits, and reported on the great hospitality she and Mademoiselle Strömsten had received when attending a training course at Nääs in Sweden. In 1903 Miss Garrett left Victoria to become headmistress of a private school run by the Misses Hardy. She renamed it the Ladies' Preparatory School; it was later known as Richmond Lodge High School.[14]

The school's facilities were continually updated and expanded to keep up with changes in education. In 1901 a new science laboratory was built to meet the needs of the general science teaching and the following year physical science was introduced. This meant that Victoria was well prepared for the new scientific examination introduced by the Department of Agriculture and Technical Institution for Ireland in 1905, while other schools struggled to cope. Cookery and needlework had long been integral to the school timetable, but in 1906 a domestic science department was established. This comprised a well-equipped kitchen with a workroom adjacent for teaching and sewing. Mrs Byers, ever keen to maximise resources

Early science laboratories, c.1908

and promote learning, invited Miss Young of the Belfast Cookery School to give weekly demonstrations in the new department to former pupils and interested ladies.[15]

The pupils always greatly enjoyed hockey and Victoria College was one of the first girls' schools in Ireland to have a hockey club. It was formed in 1896 and later joined the Northern Hockey Union, so the club could play teams from across Ireland. The team had a rather inauspicious start and lost its first match to Alexandra College, Dublin, 11–0, but improvement came swiftly and Victoria often won the Schools' Cup thereafter. At first the girls simply used the tennis courts for hockey practice, but in 1900 they benefited greatly from the generosity of Mr Forster Green of Derryvolgie House, Belfast, who offered the school land on the Malone Road, rent free, for use as a hockey pitch. Mrs Byers, Miss Matier and other supporters of the school organised the construction of a pavilion on the site.[16]

Extracurricular activities provided an opportunity for the girls to mix with pupils of all ages and backgrounds and to 'lead or to follow according to taste and capacity'.[17] The girls were given great freedom to run their own societies and games, as this was considered important for self-development. A variety of societies was formed to encourage learning in a more congenial environment and develop a sense of responsibility for the welfare of others. The Reading Society, like the Crescent Literary Society, was for girls over eighteen years of age. Members paid a yearly subscription and were obliged to uphold the thirteen rules of the society. They promised to devote an hour a day to appropriate reading and were fined a penny for any day missed. At the end of the year each member submitted to the editor a list of books she had read, excluding those she was studying in class since the society's aim was to

'The crown before us'   35

broaden the girls' knowledge of literature. Other societies included the Christian Endeavour Society, the Temperance Association, the Debating Society, the Bible Reading Union and the Missionary Meeting. The Ministering Children's League was introduced *c.*1888 and taught members to be unselfish and to learn consideration for the poor. It made donations to the Children's Hospital and a mission school in the East, and raised money for the building fund for Shamrock Lodge (another of Mrs Byers' chariable interests; see p.42), a home for destitute children in Lagan Village, Belfast.[18]

The girls were encouraged to use their holidays to travel and improve their foreign language skills. They had the chance to attend courses organised by the University of Edinburgh in Austria, France, Germany, Italy, Spain and Switzerland. There were also opportunities to work as language assistants or au pairs.[19] One former pupil, Beatrice Grimshaw (d.1953), became a renowned novelist, anthropologist and explorer. She wrote a number of fiction and non-fiction works including a comic novel, *The Victorian Family Robinson.* During her school days at Victoria College, Beatrice contributed several poems to the school magazine. Beatrice travelled extensively in the South Pacific (see below). She wrote:

> I had so many adventures that they cease to seem adventures. In the New Hebrides I was caught in a forest fire, and barely escaped into a valley where bones of a recent cannibal feast lay blackening in the smoke. […]I was present at a dance of murderers and man-eaters up in the Tanna hills, where no man went. There and elsewhere I managed to make friends with the wild men of the woods. In the Solomons, of recent years, I came in contact with the amazing native magic of the sorcerer, and lived in a house that was haunted by ghostly birds. […] I was received by the natives of Dutch New Guinea with a curious ceremony, staged as well as Hollywood could have done it – knives and spears threateningly held up by some of the younger men, while older men raised high above them a burning brand and a branch of palms, signifying homes and hearths and peace. They did not allow women to see the interior of men's temples; but I had bought my way in with a gift of bread and butter. […] I was the first white woman to ascend the Fly and Sepik, those wonderful and mysterious rivers, still little known; and only two or three white men had been before me. On the Sepik, I had my narrowest escape when a body of head-hunters urged me to come and see their village, all by myself, because their women wanted to look at me. I ventured to leave the men of my party – two only, but well armed – as I wanted greatly to see something that no one else had seen. […] the head-hunters, when they had brought out two or three old and terrified women as a bait, began to bar me into the house, while the women, hurriedly, disappeared – an unmistakable sign of trouble. I got away by backing down the track and making signals to invisible (and non-existent) friends. Head-hunters are nervy folk, jumpy and undecided until the moment when they strike. Before they had made up their minds, I was round the corner; going slowly, afterwards I ran. They had never seen a long-haired head before and there was little doubt they intended to secure that choice specimen for their head house.[20]

BEATRICE GRIMSHAW

A COMMERCIAL ENTERPRISE:
THE FINANCING OF THE SCHOOL

Mrs Byers is the Atlas upon whose shoulders this world of education
is allowed to rest. […] Just consider the circumstances. There is no
funded capital in connection with this institution, no annual endowment
accruing to it, no pile of public buildings provided for its purposes by any
public body or by the funds of the State. There is no board of managers,
no counsel or assistance or encouragement given to Mrs Byers in her
management of the institution […] We should take measures that this
should not continue and for myself I can say that, if the efforts of one
person at least can avail to bring about a more adequate recognition of
the worth and claims of Victoria College, that effort will be made.
CHARLES C. CONNOR[21]

The success of Victoria College was entirely dependent upon Mrs Byers' initiative,
determination and fearlessness. Indeed, as the Right Honourable James Stanfield declared in
1874, Mrs Byers' sole capital was her brain, for she had no endowment or board of governors.
Furthermore, the school was heavily taxed, whereas endowed schools were exempt from
taxation since they were registered charities. Mrs Byers claimed that this differentiation was
a considerable strain on the school and petitioned parliament in 1896 to extend the taxation
exemption to Victoria College, but to no avail.[22] Without public funding the school had to be
run as a commercial venture. Mrs Byers endeavoured to prove that this could be achieved
'with a little economy', but above all she was determined that pupils of moderate means
might receive an education so good 'that the wealthy cannot find better'.[23] Revenue was drawn
largely from school fees, although these were not excessive and, in fact, did not rise from
when Mrs Byers opened the Lower Crescent school until her death almost forty years later.
Fees were graded, and started at four guineas per annum for four- to seven-year-olds, rising
to eight guineas for pupils over the age of nine. This covered tuition in the core curriculum.
Additional fees were charged for stationery and optional extra lessons such as music, painting
and needlework, which were taught by outsiders. While Mrs Byers provided her pupils with
every opportunity by arranging experts to give instruction, she had to cover her expenses.
Discounts were given to daughters of the manse and to sisters; others were made at Mrs Byers'
discretion, for she was adamant that anyone of limited means or who had fallen on hard times
should not be denied an education.

 The establishment of the Intermediate Board in 1878 was a tremendous boost to
the school's finances, for it rewarded schools financially for pupils' passes ('results fees'),
awarded scholarships to outstanding pupils and helped with the purchase of equipment.
These grants were not large but helped towards repairs and engaging additional staff.
Mrs Byers strongly objected to the suggestion that results fees were degrading and was
emphatic that they were justly earned through hard work and diligence; not least, they
were essential to those schools whose resources were limited.[24]

The Victoria College hockey team, *c.*1905

DONATIONS AND SCHOLARSHIPS

Mrs Byers had a truly remarkable personality and […] drew around her
many talented and distinguished ladies as her supporters […] she inspired
in teachers and pupils alike love, reverence and awe.
A.S. McMORDIE[25]

Margaret Byers lobbied tirelessly on behalf of her school and attracted a number of supporters
who were keen to back her venture and be part of this 'glorious revolution'. Several of these
benefactors donated prizes and scholarships to help girls pursue their education, particularly

those who were over the age for competition in the Intermediate Board and had no other source of funding. In 1882 a group of former pupils came together to support Mrs Byers' work and ensure that the standard of women's education in Belfast would not fall behind other places in Ulster that received public help. They called themselves the Former Pupils' Association and raised money to support girls wishing to continue into tertiary education in the collegiate department. At the school's annual prize distribution in 1889 the Lord Mayor of Belfast, Charles C. Connor, paid tribute to this voluntary committee that had been inspired by devotion, loyalty and friendship to Mrs Byers and was her only source of help and support.[26]

The school also offered entrance scholarships. One recipient was Cathleen Nesbitt (d.1982), the renowned actress who was engaged to Rupert Brooke at the time of his death in the First World War. Cathleen recalled that her mother could not afford school fees but was determined her daughter should have the best education available in Belfast. Upon hearing that Mrs Byers offered generous scholarships to 'promising' girls, Mrs Nesbitt set her daughter to diligent preparation. Six weeks of hard graft paid off and a jubilant Cathleen won a scholarship to 'the best school in Ulster'.[27]

MRS BYERS AND THE WIDER WORLD: PHILANTHROPY, TEMPERANCE AND THE MISSION FIELD

Most people in the UK, and many in the Colonies and America, know of the
well-ordered College which you have created. […] What you have done in the
furtherance of the Temperance, and the aid which you so ungrudgingly give
to every form of philanthropic work, are also well known and highly appreciated.
But only those who, like us, have enjoyed the privilege of your friendship
can adequately realise the vast and silent influence that you exercise, and the
help and strength and comfort that you have brought to innumerable lives.
ANNA MATIER[28]

Margaret Byers stood at the forefront of educational reform for women, but she was also extensively involved in improving the welfare of young girls and women through her work on behalf of prisons, hospitals, the Temperance League and homes for the destitute. She retained an active interest in mission work and the school supported the missionaries from the Presbyterian Church and, in particular, the Women's Missionary Association, which was concerned with the education of women in India. From 1879 the girls sponsored a Syrian girl at the newly opened Damascus Mission School, which was run by two of Mrs Byers' former pupils. Indeed, a number of her girls and staff went on to work in the mission field and would send updates on their progress to the school magazine. Four former pupils who went on to work in China stated that they had each sought 'to reproduce the fine tradition of Victoria College, the appreciation of gifts in others' taught to them by their principal, as well as her 'dauntlessness and fine consideration'. They explained that Mrs Byers had maintained a strong interest in China and encouraged Victoria girls to help the country.[29]

Mrs Byers was described as a true suffragette, for she was committed to the promotion of women, although without violence. She was a devout Presbyterian and a founder member

Younger members of the school

of the Ladies' Temperance Union, established in the 1860s. The work of the union involved making garments for families who had agreed to abstain from alcohol, for they believed that much of the destitution and violence in Belfast was caused by drink. In 1874, the year that the new school was opened in Lower Crescent, Mrs Byers was founding secretary of the Belfast Women's Temperance Association, and she remained in post until 1895, when she became president. The association established the Prison Gate Mission for Women, a halfway house and programme of reform to help women make a fresh start after leaving prison and to shelter those who were victims of domestic violence. There was accommodation for thirty women at Tudor Lodge on the Crumlin Road, where the residents ran a small laundry to support themselves.[30]

The Temperance Association was also responsible for establishing the Victoria Homes for orphans and needy children, a number of whom were victims of their parents' drunkenness. In 1886 premises were rented at Shamrock Lodge, Lagan Village, where forty resident children were cared for until 1891, when the land was needed for commercial development. It was decided to purchase a site and Mrs Byers was instrumental in raising £3,000 to buy a 135-acre site at Ligoniel in the north of the city. She wrote passionate letters to the newspapers calling on the people of Belfast to support this venture, just as the Scots had supported William Quarrier's establishment of the Orphan Homes of Scotland, which Mrs Byers herself had visited. She suggested that those of means might donate £500 to sponsor a cottage that would house twenty girls.[31] Eventually six houses and three cottages were built; one, the Isabella M.S. Tod Cottage, was named after Mrs Byers' friend and fellow activist. An isolation ward for tuberculosis sufferers was named after Agnes Miller, a former pupil of Victoria College who had died of the disease.

The first Lady Superintendent of the Homes, Miss Acheson, was a former pupil of Mrs Byers'. Although a number of the girls had little interest or academic ability, they all attended classes at a school on site that was run by Miss Acheson and thereby acquired a basic education. They learned skills that would help them advance in life and, in addition, contributed to the daily chores. Indeed, the girls were themselves responsible for cooking, cleaning, gardening, washing and knitting; they even ran the farm, helped to make hay and tended the garden. The Victoria Homes was therefore a self-sufficient enterprise. By 1902 the Ligoniel site housed almost 120 children and accepted all girls, regardless of whether or not their parents were churchgoers, thus providing for those otherwise excluded by church organisations such as the Presbyterian Orphan Society.[32] A notable resident of the Homes was the Irish long-distance cycling champion, Isabel Woods (née Clement). Isabel and her sister stayed at the Ballysillan home for five years prior to the outbreak of the Second World War in 1939. Isabel described this as a 'good and happy' time and believed that both she and her sister benefited greatly from their experience in what was a well-run establishment. There was an emphasis on good behaviour, but the children had the freedom to run in the fields and enjoy fresh farm produce.[33]

CHARITY AT SCHOOL

To visit these young people and their teachers as often as I could, especially
of late years, has been my great recreation, and I have always tried to
interest the students educated at Victoria College in this form of Home
Mission work. In fact I have sought to make these Homes for destitute
children in Belfast a 'settlement' for the training of our educated girls in
caring for their less prosperous sisters.

MARGARET BYERS[34]

Mrs Byers believed that everyone who could ought to help those less fortunate and impressed
this upon her pupils, who were encouraged to support charity work at home and abroad. They
were particularly involved with the Victoria Homes and raised money at Christmas to buy
small gifts for the girls, such as gloves and neckties; one of the boarders donated a harmonium
which was greatly appreciated. The kindergarten organised an annual display – 'Children's
Hour' – and the proceeds were donated to the Belfast Women's Temperance Association for
the Victoria Homes. In 1890 the event was held in the Exhibition Hall at the Botanic Gardens
and raised the grand sum of £15 13s 0d.[35] The senior pupils were actively involved in the
Homes and acted as mentors to the little girls. Each formed a personal friendship with her
ward whom she would visit regularly to establish a relationship that was mutually beneficial.
The work of the Victoria Homes was especially dear to Mrs Byers. In 1905, when the staff and
pupils of Victoria College presented their principal with a sum of money to commemorate
her fifty years of service to education, she asked that this be used to set up a permanent
scholarship for the Victoria Homes, the Margaret Byers Fund. She hoped others would follow
this example and support Home Mission. The strong links forged between Victoria College
and the Victoria Homes continued until the 1980s. In 1981 the Victoria Homes admitted boys
and became the Victoria Voluntary Homes. Following the sale of its property in 1988, the
Victoria Homes Trust was established.[36] Whether she was helping destitute children at home,
girls attending a mission school in Damascus or her pupils at Victoria College, Margaret Byers'
main objective was to help them 'do their life work intelligently and well'.[37]

A LIFETIME'S ACHIEVEMENT: 'THE PRIDE AND GLORY OF THE GREAT CITY OF THE NORTH'[38]

Margaret Byers, the pride and glory of the great city of the North, who
not only there but throughout our whole island, in word and deed with
energy and wisdom, has stood in the forefront of a great and praiseworthy
revolution. Here, for fifty years, a large space in mortal life, she has stood
beside the helm with unflinching firmness having experienced storm and
calm, but with a steady mind in either fortune.

DR LOUIS CLAUDE PURSER[39]

In 1905, Mrs Byers' fiftieth year in the teaching profession, she was awarded an honorary

Margaret Byers in her doctoral robes, 1905

doctorate (LLD) by Trinity College Dublin in recognition of her outstanding services to education. She was the first woman in Ulster to be awarded an honorary degree. This was a source of great pride and honour to her staff, pupils and former students, who presented their principal with her academic robes and established a bursary in her name at the Victoria Homes. The honorary degree was a fitting tribute to a woman who had campaigned tirelessly to raise the standard of girls' education in Ireland and vehemently promoted women in the teaching profession. She had taken huge risks, courted controversy and, ultimately, silenced her critics. To her pupils and staff Dr Byers was an inspiration. Her speeches at the annual prize distributions were remembered as uplifting and moving. According to one former student she created 'a spiritual atmosphere'; she impressed upon her girls that higher education opened every door to them and that they could do anything they wished. According to Melissa Hull,

> She was herself a woman of the brain and wide human sympathies,
> broad-minded and great-hearted. She could be awe-inspiring, of course.[40]

Margaret Byers inspired respect and reverence in her pupils, but they all recalled her great warmth of character and the genuine interest she took in each of the girls; she was as concerned about their health and sporting prowess as their academic achievements. Her letters to the pupils, printed in the school magazines, are invariably addressed to 'My dear young friends' and signed 'Your friend', a reflection of the deep affection she held for the girls.

In her later years Dr Byers was dogged by ill health. Despite her infirmity, she retained an active interest in school life and endeavoured to participate as much as she could: she attended the pupils' fancy dress parties and made an appearance at the annual prize distribution. In 1955 the guest of honour at the school prize distribution was Thomas Finnegan, president of Magee University College Londonderry and also an 'old boy' of Victoria, since he had attended the kindergarten in Lower Crescent. He recalled looking across the Crescent as a boy and watching the aged headmistress being wheeled in her bath-chair; to him, she looked like Queen Victoria.[41] For the last two years of Dr Byers' life, Miss Matier, the vice principal, took over much of the running of the school and read the annual school report on her behalf. Nevertheless, Dr Byers remained 'a great and silent presence'.[42]

Dr Margaret Morrow Byers died on 21 February 1912. Her oak coffin, shrouded in her doctoral robes, lay in state in the lecture hall of Victoria College, at the heart of her empire. The Union Jack at Queen's University Belfast was lowered to half mast as a tribute to this remarkable woman, 'the pride and glory of the North', whose vision had 'passed into reality'.[43]

> Changes and improvements will, no doubt, come in education as in
> everything else and new generations, let us hope, will desire a still
> higher order of things. But when I look back on the last thirty years, so
> eventful, so full of enterprise and success and think of the pioneer work
> unaided and alone we undertook here and accomplished, am I vain if
> I regard the small space contained within these walls almost as classic
> ground which I wish to be retained and managed wisely for the good
> of future generations?
> MARGARET BYERS[44]

Drumglass House today

The Boarding Department

*A place 'where the inevitable never happens
and the unexpected frequently does'.*
MURIEL FINCH, QUOTING W.B. YEATS[45]

When Mrs Byers opened the Establishment for the Boarding and Education of Young Ladies in 1859, she made the boarding department an essential part of the school, so that girls living in remote areas of the province or whose parents worked abroad might have the same educational opportunities as local girls. Throughout its 150-year history, the boarding department has remained a fundamental part of Victoria College. Indeed, when the boarders were evacuated to Portballintrae during the Second World War, the then headmistress, Mrs Faris, claimed that the school was not quite itself and was delighted when she could welcome them back in September 1945.

Initially boarders outnumbered day girls and ensured the survival of the school at a time when Mrs Byers was little known in Belfast. Once the school was established and numbers had risen, there were generally 60 or 70 boarders and 250 day girls. These numbers were ideal if the resident staff were not to be overly burdened.[46] Today, the boarding department accommodates over sixty boarders and resident staff and represents about 5 per cent of the school's population.

The early days

Up until 1923, when it moved to Drumglass House, the boarding department was contained within the school buildings at its various sites. In the Lower Crescent school, the dormitories and bathrooms were on the second and third floors, while the dining hall with its kitchen was on the ground floor. The dormitories were divided into cubicles, but separate rooms were available at additional cost and it was not uncommon for sisters to share. In 1889 the annual residential rates, excluding tuition fees, were twenty-seven guineas for girls under eleven and thirty for those over eleven years of age. Additional charges included pew rent, laundry and medical fees. There were optional extras such as riding lessons and music tuition. Boarders were issued with a lengthy inventory listing all that they were required to bring with them. This included two pairs of sheets, six towels and table napkins, two pillowcases, two bolster cases, a spoon and two forks; knives were seemingly not mentioned. Each girl was to have a warm dressing-gown, slippers, two pairs of bed-socks and a bed-jacket to combat the chill. The dormitories could be noisy at night and one former pupil recalled how the whole building would shake when heavy-goods trains went by.[47]

The boarders tended to forge strong friendships with each other and while they joined the day girls for lessons and societies after school, they generally socialised together and formed their own separate group. There was no weekly boarding at this time and the girls therefore spent their weekends at the school, although most returned home during the holidays. A few remained for the entire year if, for example, their parents were missionaries or their homes were remote. They might be treated to a theatre visit to liven up the holiday period.

In 1959 the Centenary Committee interviewed several women who had been boarders during Dr Byers' headship. Annie McMordie (d.1959) outlined their daily routine at this time, which began with breakfast in the dining room. This was followed by prayers and bed-making. The boarders joined the rest of the school for assembly at 9 a.m. All pupils had a break at 11 a.m. and the boarders were served dinner at 3 p.m. Those who had no afternoon classes then went for a walk, either up the Malone or Stranmillis roads; they marched two by two in the customary 'croc', with the tallest at the front and the smallest at the back. These walks were particularly lively after a snowfall when the Victoria croc was likely to be ambushed by a group of boys from Methodist College, who lay in wait for their target. But the girls took this in good spirits and regarded it an 'hilarious and exciting experience'.[48] The two native language assistants, the Mademoiselle and the Fräulein, were resident members of staff and were actively involved with the boarders. They usually led the croc, and while the older pupils would practise their languages, the younger girls would be entertained by fairy stories from the Brothers Grimm or Hans Christian Andersen. Mealtimes offered a further opportunity for the senior girls to improve their languages, since they would take it in turns to sit beside the language assistants and practise their conversation. A light supper was served at 6 p.m. and was followed by study time known as 'prep'. The girls worked until 8.30 p.m. and were then free to dance in the lecture hall or play the piano and worried little about the noise they made. The younger girls went to bed at 9 p.m., while the older pupils were permitted to stay up until 11 p.m.[49]

On Saturday mornings the boarders had a geometrical drawing class with Miss Steele, but were free in the afternoons to visit friends or relatives. Melissa Hull remembered one occasion when she had hoped to go to a cricket match with her brother at Campbell College. He sent her the details in a coded message, with the words written backwards in French. Mrs Byers was not so easily fooled and when Melissa arrived to collect her mail, the headmistress explained that there had been a measles epidemic at Campbell and she should not handle the card lest she caught and spread the infection. With a twinkle in her eye Mrs Byers 'gingerly' held up the letter to the mirror 'by two

The boarding department, c.1910

A double Cubicle

A dormitory in the Lower Crescent school

extremities' so that Melissa could decipher the message in the glass. Melissa realised that there would be no cricket match that day.[50]

On Sunday mornings Mrs Byers would review the girls' behaviour and mention anything 'unworthy of Victoria College standards' that had been brought to her attention. Fines were duly imposed and the proceeds given to the Damascus Mission. The minister of Fisherwick was clearly confused about the origins of this money for on one occasion when the donation was considerably larger than usual the delighted clergyman heartily thanked the girls for their splendid efforts.[51] The girls attended church, either Presbyterian (Fisherwick) or Church of Ireland (St Thomas's). Sunday afternoons were devoted to Mrs Byers' Bible-study class. The girls were expected to learn several verses, but this was not an arduous task and as several pupils noted, they memorised some of the most beautiful passages that they could still recall and always greatly treasured. Although

most came well prepared, a few who had been remiss would feign illness to escape humiliation.

While Mrs Byers was a great advocate of higher education, she believed that all aspects of the character should be developed and organised a number of social events for the boarders, who also helped with her charity work and gave concerts in the lecture hall to raise money for good causes. The boarders were invited to the 'at homes' Mrs Byers periodically held to raise money for charity. These took place in the lecture hall which was carpeted and transformed into a drawing room. An invited dignitary addressed the guests and the older girls then served tea while music was played in the background. The boarders greatly relished these events, particularly the tea and cakes that were served in abundance. Occasionally they enjoyed at homes with their brothers from the Royal Belfast Academical Institution (RBAI), who were invited to tea and for parlour games. They in turn were treated to tea with the principal of RBAI and were invariably invited to any dance celebrating the boys' success on the sports field.[52]

Trips to the theatre were a particular treat. When Sir Frank Benson's company visited for its annual season, the boarders were allowed to attend any Shakespeare play they were studying. On their return from these special outings the girls were accorded the rare privilege of using Mrs Byers' private entrance and were given warm milk and biscuits by the parlour-maid. There was great excitement one year when Sir Frank and his company used Victoria's hockey pitch to take on the Queen's College, Belfast. The girls were equally thrilled when Sir Frank swept off his hat when he met them on the street.[53]

Events of national and local significance made a deep impact. E. Maud Farrington (née White) from Cork was a boarder in the final years of Dr Byers' 'reign'. She recalled vividly the memorial service for Edward VII in 1910, at which the boarders paraded 'in truly royal mourning'. Their clothes had been dyed for the occasion, but as this had been done rather too swiftly and en masse, their garments were more purple than black. Nevertheless the girls managed to remain dignified and sombre.[54] Laura Patterson (née Wood) remembered the Crescent Presbyterian Church opposite the school burning down in the winter of 1918, when Miss Matier was headmistress of the school. All the girls were evacuated in the middle of the night lest the flames spread, but, fortunately, there were no casualties and the school was not damaged. Nothing further was ever said about the cause of the fire, although the girls later learned it had been arson.[55]

The resident staff

In the late nineteenth century the boarding department was run by the matron, Miss Woods, who ruled 'with kindly sway' and had an ageing band of helpers in tow. Cook appeared once a year on Shrove Tuesday when the girls presented her with a pair of new kid gloves, although none of the boarders seemed to know the origins of this tradition. One character who made a deep impression was Sarah, the one-legged boot lady who 'dwelt in a cavernous subterranean domain, pigeon-holed from floor to ceiling'. The girls went to the boot hall twice a day to change their shoes, and the younger ones were uncertain, if not terrified of old Sarah. According to Melissa Hull:

> when the horde swept down on her with clatter and babel, [Sarah] would rise from her stool in a cloud of dust, brandish what must have been her walking stick, but which I, as a small and terrified new girl, imagined to be her wooden leg, and bellow in stentorian tones, 'The Boot Hall must be REDD'.[56]

Melissa, who was not from the North, had no idea what this in fact meant, but years later learned that 'redd' meant 'cleared up' or 'put in order'.

Drumglass House: 'the land of scholars and the nurse of souls'[57]

In 1922 the board of governors purchased Drumglass House, the former home of the businessman and benefactor, Sir Henry Musgrave. This was largely at the instigation of Miss Matier, who wanted to provide the resident pupils with a country environment in the town, where they could run off their energies. The move was also a necessity, for numbers had continued to rise in the school and the building was struggling to accommodate all the pupils; the boarders' quarters were thus needed for classrooms. The 'secluded and quiet' setting of Drumglass House was remodelled under Miss Matier's direction and in September 1923 it opened as a residence. It has remained the boarders' home ever since.

Life in the boarding department was closely regulated. For example, no tuck boxes were allowed, although a little ripe fruit was permitted on occasion, and all pocket money was to be given into the custody of the housemistress. Kathleen Davey (née Burrows) was a boarder in the 1930s and was, in fact, the first weekly boarder. Her father had negotiated this special and unprecedented arrangement so that Kathleen would not have to make the daily journey from east

i A group of boarders at the door of Drumglass House, *c*.1930

ii The Victoria croc prepares to 'proceed rapidly onwards' to Lower Crescent, 1933

iii Thespians of Drumglass, *c*.1930

Belfast, but could return to her family at the weekends. She thus had the best of both worlds. Kathleen was fifteen when she arrived at Drumglass in 1933 and was shown to her cubicle – 'a small basic room with walls two feet short of the ceiling'. The girls had privacy but could still communicate with their comrades and anyone 'sufficiently determined' might crawl along the top of the partition and drop down into her neighbour's room. Each day followed a definite structure and began with breakfast in the dining room, where the seniors and juniors sat at separate tables. The girls then formed the habitual croc to walk to Lower Crescent, and returned in the same manner in the afternoon. There was a short time to play before prep; anyone who finished early was to read a novel quietly. Afterwards, the girls practised music, danced in the hall and partook of the staple Drumglass fare – sliced white bread. Matron said prayers before bed and lights out was at 9.30 p.m. for seniors. Miss Matier was warden of Drumglass when Kathleen was a boarder and she took a keen interest in the goings on there; indeed, she introduced puffed wheat to break the monotony of porridge for breakfast.[58]

Mary Balfour (née Lindsay) joined Drumglass as a boarder in January 1939 and recalls that her first year was spent in the pink dormitory; thereafter she progressed to the blue dormitory. While Mary was homesick at first, she later enjoyed her time at Drumglass; she remembered a trip to the Opera House, which was her first experience of the theatre, and her weekend visits to her grandmother, the Reverend Edith Martin.[59]

The post-war years

There was nothing of the earth mother about the Resident Headmistress but she had a great understanding of teenage girls … she believed in as few rules as possible. Drumglass was a happy place, orderly and, by the standards of the time, liberal.

ROMAYNE CARSWELL (NÉE FERRIS)[60]

During the Second World War Drumglass House was requisitioned by the government and the entire boarding department was evacuated to Portballintrae (see pp. 84–7). The girls returned to Drumglass in September 1945 and their warden, Miss Hogg, helped them adjust to their new surroundings. She also restored Drumglass to its former glory, a considerable task which 'bore a resemblance to the Augean Stables'. Miss Hogg 'ruled supreme in her fiefdom' until her retirement in 1968 and is remembered as a strict yet liberal-minded warden who had a great sense of humour and a number of eccentricities. Her hairstyle and dress seemed rather dated to the girls and many of her phrases were 'idiosyncratic' – in the mornings she would command the Drumglass croc to 'proceed rapidly onwards' to Lower Crescent. Former colleagues recall the cigarette that would dangle from her mouth, although this was probably kept well hidden from the girls. While Miss Hogg presided over Drumglass 'with a confidence and confidence-inspiring sureness', she had a nervous habit of buttoning and unbuttoning the waistcoats of visiting parents, who were justifiably a little perturbed by this performance. But Miss Hogg was above all a tolerant and capable warden who was devoted to her 'little daisies'.[61]

Astrid Maddocks (née McMath) was one of the Portballintrae boarders who arrived at Drumglass in September 1945. She was struck by the vastness of the grounds and soon developed a liking for climbing the trees. Astrid remembers the morning walk to Lower Crescent in the croc, which was ideal for memory work; the great enjoyment of Miss Brazil's dance classes; and the occasion when her Classics teacher, Mrs Phillips, invited all the boarders to a sumptuous tea at her house. Less popular was the stale sandwich of bread and margarine that each boarder was given for 11 a.m. break along with a bottle of free milk. One of Astrid's final memories was the midnight feast she and her accomplices planned as their farewell to Drumglass. The music room was the scene of the crime and the girls giggled and munched their way through the night. The following morning at breakfast the reprobates were understandably

Miss Rita Hogg, *c*.1930

rather peaky and struggled with their food. Matron said nothing but she, 'who always knew everything', looked on with amusement.[62]

Emily Hunter joined the boarding department in 1947 and recalls their weekend activities. Saturday mornings were spent sewing and darning – a necessity in the post-war years – but they took walks on the Lagan towpath in the afternoons and looked forward to their annual trip to the Ideal Home Exhibition.[63]

When Miss Ann Williams (Mrs Morrison) was appointed head of PE in 1966, she was required to reside in Drumglass House and assist with boarding duties. At the weekends this meant escorting the croc to Fisherwick for the morning and evening services. The boarders were generally impeccably behaved, but they had their moments. Ann recalls one such occasion when her charges amused themselves during the service by tying together their scarves. They were duly reprimanded from the pulpit by the Reverend Jack Withers, who was also a member of the board of governors.[64]

Two young boarders enjoy French conversation with Mademoiselle Christiane Baudin, *News Letter*, 10 January 1963

Recent times and new developments

1987 will be an historic year in the diary of Drumglass as it will witness the loss [...] of Miss Finch, our guardian angel who has admirably guided many a young Victorian though her school life with unprecedented success.

UPPER-SIXTH BOARDERS[65]

Miss Muriel Finch was appointed warden of Drumglass in 1968 and presided as the 'guardian angel' of the boarding department until 1987. She was a strong and colourful character who made a deep impression on the many girls who passed through Drumglass – and also on their parents. Miss Finch has left her imprint literally across the globe and over the years attended many birthday parties, weddings, christenings and anniversaries in a number of countries. 'Her girls' have vivid memories of their time at Drumglass and of their mentor who prepared them for life after school.[66] Caroline Young (née Lusk) recalls her wonderful sense of humour and love of life, which she passed on to the boarders, and the reassurance she gave, particularly to those who were fretting over examination results. Miss Finch would impress upon them that their common sense would take them much farther than brains. While those who left Drumglass regarded Miss Finch as a friend, to the younger girls she was a formidable disciplinarian who believed that privileges were to be earned through age and experience. Thus, the younger girls were subject to strict regulations and were expected to show respect to the senior girls. However, they knew that later, having served their apprenticeship, they would reap the benefits. Indeed, the climax of every boarder's 'career' was her invitation to Miss Finch's supper party in her final year, where she was groomed for the world beyond Drumglass.[67]

Discipline was the first lesson that the boarder learned in Drumglass. Miscreants were sent by matron to stand outside Miss Finch's office, and they waited nervously, fearful of their warden's imminent return. But this was an effective deterrent, for anyone who had stood at that door did not want to repeat the experience. Despite the rules there was much fun and

Miss Finch and her girls, 1987

Entrance hall of
Drumglass House with
its Victorian tiled floor

hilarity. One of Caroline Young's happiest memories is of 'sun bathing à la Drumglass', when the girls basted themselves in butter, lay on tinfoil and relaxed in the sun. Caroline recalls that Miss Finch was furious when she discovered them and was probably as concerned about the sight and smell of the buttered girls as the implications for their health.[68] The highlight of the boarders' year was the Christmas party, particularly the after-dinner entertainment, which featured plays that were often 'as hilarious as they were unrehearsed'. This is still a greatly anticipated event in Drumglass and is attended by the headmistress.[69]

In 1973 the upper-sixth boarders wrote the first of their annual reports for *The Victorian*. Charting the highs and lows of life in Drumglass, these reports convey the sense of community spirit in the boarding department and the girls' fondness for the resident staff, particularly their warden. They note the various privileges accorded, such as permission to wear trousers after school and the introduction of toast for supper. They record structural changes, notably the formation of a boarders' committee in 1982 and the appointment of a head boarder in 1987. The reports also offer an insight into the impact of the Troubles on Drumglass. Bomb scares in the middle of the night would see a band of 'sixty-five sodden-slippered refugees' arrive at Mrs Berner's house, where they were consoled with a large tin of Quality Street. Mrs Berner recalls one occasion when there was snow on the ground and the older girls carried the younger ones on their backs.[70]

Miss Finch's retirement from Drumglass marked the end of an era in the boarding department and was particularly regretted by those who had served their time as juniors and never reaped the rewards of their endeavours. In 1997 a magnolia tree was planted outside Drumglass House in memory of a much-loved warden and teacher of art.

Miss Finch was succeeded first by Janice Flinn (1987–91), and thereafter by Margaret McVeigh (1991–9), Heather Rendell (1999–2004) and Joanne Brown (2004–7). Helen Robinson has held office since 2007. Various activities have been introduced over the

years, initiated by the wardens and matrons or at the request of the girls. They include weekend hikes in the Mournes; classes in ballroom dancing, cookery, aerobics and first aid; the formation of a sub-aqua and snorkelling club; and an annual visit to support the Belfast Giants Ice Hockey team. One evening a week the girls have exclusive use of the school's swimming pool and can avail themselves of the school library and computer network outside class hours. Themed evenings offer an opportunity to celebrate and explore the cultures of foreign boarders and resident staff. The welcoming in of the Chinese New Year is a particular highlight and Drumglass is duly adorned with red banners bearing messages of goodwill. There is an opportunity to develop teamwork and leadership skills, and to collaborate with other schools. Indeed, an exchange operates between Drumglass and the boarders of Rathmore, Dublin.

Drumglass remains a truly cosmopolitan home and accommodates pupils and resident staff from across the globe. It continues to provide a temporary home for language assistants and in recent years has welcomed a number of exchange students and staff.

Halloween in the boarding department

Reconstitution as a public school

Victoria College under Miss Matier, 1912–30

Miss Anna Matier

That wonderful woman Mrs Byers founded the school
but it was Miss Matier who built up the whole superstructure
of Victoria College and raised it to a position of eminence.

THE RIGHT HONOURABLE H. POLLOCK[1]

In April 1912, two months after Margaret Byers' death, the future of the school was uncertain. Miss Anna Matier, who was vice principal and acting head of Victoria College, was notified by solicitors representing Dr Byers' son and heir, Sir John, that he felt unable to commit to continuing the school. They hoped that Victoria College would be bought as a going concern and that the new owner would retain the current staff. But this was not guaranteed and it was an anxious time for the teachers who, having lost their principal, were now faced with the prospect of losing their jobs and livelihood.

Many of the teachers were former pupils of the school and shared Dr Byers' vision and determination. They were adamant that Victoria College should continue as their founder had intended and suggested an arrangement whereby they would take on the role of tenants on a trial basis, paying an annual rent of £150 to Sir John and accepting all responsibilities for the running of the school. This plucky response was a tribute to Margaret Byers, who had inspired such loyalty and commitment. However, their proposal was rejected. Instead it was decided that a small company should be formed to own the school, which would be under the management of the headmistress, Miss Matier. A loan was secured and Victoria College Limited was established.

The school now became a public venture rather than a private enterprise and was, in fact, the first public girls' school in Ulster.[2] The company comprised a small committee of 'local friends of education' and included Dr Byers' daughter-in-law, Lady Byers (d.1950), who subsequently became a governor of the school until 1936, when she moved to Newcastle. In 1946 her son, Frank Byers, the youngest grandson of the founder, joined the board.[3] The restructuring of the school was acknowledged by the Department of Agriculture in February 1913 and anticipated the monumental changes consequent to the formation of Northern Ireland, the establishment of the Ministry of Education for Northern Ireland and the promulgation of the 1923 Education Act.

In 1918 Sir John Byers paid tribute to his mother's ability to select workers; others referred to her as an 'unerring judge of character'.[4] Certainly, it was the loyalty of the teaching staff and the determination of Miss Matier that ensured the school's survival at this time, and its subsequent success. Shortly after its reconstitution, the new headmistress was able to note, with pride, that numbers were rising, attendance was at an all-time high, the examination results were outstanding and the girls were in good health. Moreover, the school had received positive reports in a recent inspection. Victoria College, with its staff of thirty-two graduates and specialists, was advertised as offering 'a wide and liberal education, preparatory to university studies', with training in cooking, secretarial work and all branches of housecraft. The school was well equipped with a house for boarders, laboratories, a gymnasium and sports field, for, as Miss Matier declared, 'one learns in Victoria College not only how to work but how to play'.[5] Victoria College thus continued as 'a centre of thorough and liberal education' that promoted academic excellence and created a foundation for good citizenship.[6]

MISS ANNA MATIER:
'A TYRANT AND A FAIRY GODMOTHER'[7]

She ruled as an autocrat her little world, the world of school.

NORAH WATTS[8]

Miss Anna Matier had been a resident pupil at the Ladies' Collegiate and was subsequently co-opted on to the staff by her principal, Margaret Byers. From 1908 she served as vice principal and in Dr Byers' final years was chiefly responsible for the running of the school; indeed, she was the founder's designated successor. Following her appointment as headmistress in 1912, Miss Matier stepped down from teaching to devote herself to the administration of the school, which was at this time the largest and most prominent girls' school in Ulster.

Miss Matier regarded education as 'a journey along a congenial and companionable road' rather than a cold, austere duty, and she was remembered by former pupils as an inspiring and charismatic teacher whose history and literature lessons were 'works of art'.[9] However, Miss Matier later confessed that she considered mathematics a most difficult subject – while Ruskin claimed that every girl should pursue one branch of knowledge until it led her 'to the bitter valley of Humiliation', she reckoned that with mathematics, this threshold was quickly reached.[10]

Colleagues and pupils remarked on Miss Matier's 'irrepressible sense of humour' and optimism. She was diminutive but indomitable, sharp-witted and engaging, but could be extremely cutting and made a delinquent feel 'a mere worm'. She was truly the 'Benevolent Despot'.[11] Pupils recalled Miss Matier's regal bearing and immaculate dress that set her apart from the other teachers and appealed to the girls, who stood in awe of this alluring autocrat whom they feared and adored in equal measure. As one former student explained, she was a remarkable woman and one you would never forget, 'let alone argue with. All four feet six inches, she could hold her own with anyone half as tall again.'[12]

> The Miss Matier you know built a new school on the foundations of the old; the Miss Matier we knew built us a new world. Such callow youngsters we were when we came to her, Cinderellas of fourteen suddenly confronted with a mixture of a tyrant and a fairy godmother, who made us, as far as our sensations went, at one moment into toads and one next into princesses. She dragooned us into manners; she mocked us into common sense; and she taught us history. Or rather she was history. She was the eighteenth-century incarnate; she was Charles I flinging open the doors of the House to arrest the five members; and hers was every arrogant head that went to the guillotine in 1793. I am sorry to say she never had any sympathy for rebels against properly constituted authority. None of us leaving her had anything to learn about absolute monarchy. Historians still marvel at the secret of Elizabeth that one so arbitrary, so whimsical, so feminine, so despotic could command such absolute adoration; we never marvelled. We had known Elizabeth. But she gave us more than a sense of the past; she gave us faith in the future; or rather her faith in our future. […] She was, and thank heaven is still a gallant and obstinate lover of life.
>
> HELEN WADDELL[13]

DAILY LIFE

And why beholdest thou the mote that is in thy brother's eye but regardest
not the beam that is in thine own eye?
MATTHEW 7:3

Like Dr Byers before her, Miss Matier played a prominent part in school life. She led the daily assembly in the lecture hall at Lower Crescent and at 9.30 a.m. the girls would invariably hear the words of Matthew 7:3 'spoken with decisive enunciation though little sweetness'.[14] Miss Matier visited each class to take the daily roll call and would stride majestically into the classroom armed with the register. This was 'the most thrilling moment' of the girls' day, for they never knew whether to expect praise or blame; Miss Matier was totally unpredictable and thoroughly compelling.[15] A babbling throng of girls was silenced immediately by the mere appearance of their headmistress, each pupil fearful that the 'slightly-hooded eye' was staring right at her and that the 'frail but resonant voice' would make a quip about her uniform or posture, for Miss Matier's long experience in the classroom had given her 'the power of suggesting, to an uncanny degree, an all-knowing mind behind an all-seeing eye'. Yet the girls cherished any encounter they had with their awe-inspiring principal and enjoyed her witty conversation. She did not reserve her bon mots for the urbane, but enchanted even the youngest girls with her incisive remarks about men and the world. Elizabeth Bishop, who was a pupil in the 1920s, explained that although she had undoubtedly learned many things from her headmistress, what stood out most in her mind was Miss Matier's insistence that she stop interpolating every sentence with 'You see'.[16]

While Miss Matier was at times autocratic towards the older girls, she was extremely fond of the younger children, whom she visited regularly, and she always had funny comments to make.[17] Once the girls left the preparatory school, they were disciplined rather than indulged, and serious offences provoked the principal to great anger; in extreme cases, her voice would tremble. Yet it seemed to the girls that their lighter antics were almost appreciated by their principal:

> Although no one could be sterner than she when some hurtful trick
> was practised, I am sure that some of us retain to this day a fond, if foolish
> pride that some of our pranks met, not with punishment but rather with
> whimsical appreciation from our headmistress.[18]

Pupils and colleagues paid tribute to Miss Matier's concern for her pupils, whom she knew by name and track record. While Miss Matier took tremendous delight in the academic achievements of her girls, it was the weaker pupils who received her particular attention and were given time and devotion.[19] She worried about the girls' health and welfare as much as their academic achievement and was even troubled about the warmth of their underwear. When school dinners were introduced for day girls, Miss Matier checked the menus herself to ensure they were well balanced. Nothing was deemed too trivial or menial, although she was not good at delegating and 'held all the strings in her own hands'.[20]

Miss Matier maintained a passionate interest in former pupils, who would visit to seek her advice, show their babies or simply to share their news. Helen Waddell, the distinguished medievalist and writer, formed a particularly close relationship with Miss Matier, whom she fondly dubbed 'Her Majesty'. She explained that Miss Matier always kept abreast of her girls' achievements: 'no event occurs in the career of her former pupils that does not bring in its wake some message of encouragement or congratulation from Miss Matier'. When Helen was a student of the newly constituted Queen's University Belfast, she would visit Miss Matier, then vice principal of Victoria College, and she recalled one occasion when the 'little lady' gave her money to buy a new outfit:

> Madame eyed me up: the next I heard of it was a cheque for five
> guineas and a command plus entreaty to go to Lowry's and buy
> me a respectable garment. That little lady would like to dress me in
> a Field-of-Cloth-of-Gold manner, and feed me on curds and cream, and
> marry me to the Prince of Wales. She told me once that I did not know
> how much I mattered to her; and that is why I can let her do things
> like this. The result is an exquisite Shantung silk coat and skirt, a deep
> creamy yellow: very soft and full, with a broad sailor collar. And with
> it – this was extravagant – an enormous black hat.[21]

A LIVING INSTITUTION

Victoria College was a vibrant and dynamic institution under Miss Matier's direction. Prize days, 'the recurring decimal of the scholastic year', must have been eagerly anticipated by parents and pupils alike, for the principal was an eloquent and engaging orator whose speeches were witty, entertaining and always unpredictable. In 1919 Miss Matier referred to the difficult task of keeping her staff from matrimony and referred to five 'backsliders' that year. She could be scathing, but also self-deprecating, and described the preparation of the annual school report 'a little like the Fast Days of the old Scots Kirk, a sort of spiritual stock-taking'; those whom the process did not 'lead through the Valley of Humiliation' were 'singularly fortunate or peculiarly obstinate'. On one occasion, when the chair of the board complimented Miss Matier on how well she was looking, she tersely replied, 'Mutton dressed as lamb'.[22] This wit and humour pervaded school life, and whoever happened to cross the principal's path was likely to encounter her quick tongue. One Students' Day, a crowd of boys burst into the school and met Miss Matier in the hall. She quipped, 'Gentlemen, you have made a mistake. This is not the recruiting office.' A rather large and robust father who objected to following Miss Matier's rules declared he could put the tiny headmistress in his pocket, which elicited the warning, 'Yes, and you'd be jolly glad to let her out again.'[23]

Miss Matier was supported by a staff of colourful and even eccentric characters who were remembered with fondness. Miss Steele, who had been a pupil at the school and was English mistress for over forty years, was a great and inspiring teacher who encouraged independence of thought and action. Colleagues recalled her witty and engaging conversation as 'she held her court' each morning in the staff cloakroom, regaling her listeners with an incisive report on the latest news. Miss Matier and she did not, evidently, get along. Mary Rogers (née Morwood), who was a pupil in the 1920s, explained that although the two women respected each other, there was clearly no love lost between them. The girls had an interesting

i   Miss Barnes, 1927

ii   Miss Matier with Tommy and friends at Ballygalley, *c*.1930

iii Mademoiselle Oppliger

iv Miss Carson at staff hockey match, *c*.1920

v   Members of staff at the school sports day, 1922

theory as to why this was so, which Mary considered was probably fanciful, and she did not provide details when recounting her memories in 1959. But Mary did believe that it had been an important lesson for her to realise that adults did not necessarily get along, and that she could like them both despite, or perhaps because of, their differences.[24]

Another memorable character was Mr George Smith, the music teacher, 'an original in his own way'. Mr Smith was a great pianist and would sometimes treat the girls to a concert after class. He frequently wrote hockey songs to spur on the team and was a regular supporter at matches, when he would don the school colours and cheer on the Victoria players. Mr Smith was remembered as a dedicated teacher who always had a smile on his face and would invariably be seen clutching his muffler, overcoat and stick. He was seemingly undaunted by the sea of females that surrounded him and was an integral part of Victoria College for over twenty-five years. Mr Smith retired from the staff in 1943 and died shortly thereafter; his wife established a school scholarship in his memory.[25]

Other remarkable figures included Hilda Johnston, the elocution teacher who would stride around the school in her furs and hat, and Miss Barnes, from England, from whom the girls learned 'the possibilities of sarcasm'. However, it was Miss Matier, tiny, 'erect, white-haired and supremely self-confident', who was the 'dominating presence' in the school.[26]

THE OUTBREAK OF WAR

Outwardly the surface of school life has not much altered; one would hardly have it otherwise with those 'waters blown by winds to laughter and lit by the rich skies all day'.
ANNA MATIER[27]

At the annual prize distribution in June 1914, Miss Matier reported on the school's success and progress. Several weeks later the world was at war and Victoria College was confronted with an unprecedented situation. The headmistress' yearly reports during the war years offer a vivid and often poignant insight into the war's impact on the school, particularly on its morale. As Miss Matier noted in 1918, they feared that the world had been turned upside down, yet feared that there would not be change in the end, for they did 'not want to see again the world before the war'.[28]

School life continued with a semblance of normality. In the Intermediate Board examinations Victoria College maintained its accustomed position as the leading girls' school in Ireland; indeed, 1918 was deemed an exceptional year. Sport and exercise remained an essential part of the daily regime. Basketball and hockey were played in winter, and in 1915 the team won the Ulster Schools' Hockey Cup. Tennis was enjoyed in summer on the four hard and four grass courts. The girls received instruction in British and Swedish drill as well as deportment and dancing. On Saturday mornings they attended swimming and diving lessons. The school inspection was favourable and attendance had risen, as indeed was the case at schools throughout Belfast during this period. The *Northern Whig* suggested that this was a direct consequence of the war, for people were seemingly concerned to have an education and a future, and to fill the void left in universities.[29]

Nevertheless the imprint of the war pervaded the school. The pupils knitted socks for soldiers and agreed to give up their prizes and donate the book money to 'the relief of our gallant soldiers and sailors'. Miss Matier explained that it was easier 'to face life with an empty bookshelf where the prizes ought to be than with an empty sleeve'. Hence, during the war years certificates were awarded in lieu of books. The girls staged annual 'patriotic entertainments' to raise money. Two such events organised in December 1914 helped the Belfast Motor Ambulance Fund and the Hospital for Limbless Soldiers.[30] By the end of the war Victoria College had contributed £1,020 to the war effort. Former pupils were involved in all aspects of war work. Details of their service and achievements were duly reported in the annual school reports and, from 1916, in the school magazine, *The Victorian*. In 1917 Miss Matier paid particular tribute to the sculptress and former pupil, Anne Acheson, whose invention of the papier-mâché splint had done so much to ease the agony of soldiers and who was, she remarked, a wonderful example of 'the Artist as servant of the State'.[31] Perhaps the most poignant reminder of the war in these 'dark days' was the absence of a pupil every few weeks because a brother had been posted dead or missing.[32]

A CHANGED WORLD: THE POST-WAR YEARS AND EDUCATIONAL REFORM

To us, as to the eight saved souls looking out from the Ark, the face of the earth is very dry. [...] Meanwhile, Victoria College has something of the mood that remembered there were brave men before Agamemnon – it has seen good years before the passing of the Education Act, even if, after it, it hopes to see better. [...] The fate of Irish education will be decided as it always has been by the quality of the work done daily in the schools. The problem of the State is in the end the problem of the individual personality.
ANNA MATIER[33]

The post-war years brought significant change to Ireland and its schools. Following the Government of Ireland Act in 1920, which partitioned the country and set up two parliaments – one in Dublin and one in Belfast – and the subsequent creation of Northern Ireland, Victoria College entered into an agreement with the newly established Ministry of Education for Northern Ireland and came under its aegis in March 1922. This meant that the school now received government funding and was financially secure for the first time in its history. A 'fully-fledged' board of governors of ten members under Mr Hugh Pollock, the Minister of Finance for Northern Ireland, replaced the small committee that had hitherto run the school, and a new company was formed.[34] As a consequence of this, and indeed of the school's earlier relationship with the Department of Agriculture, Victoria College was little affected by changes introduced by and subsequent to the Education Act of 1923. The Act was initiated by Lord Londonderry, Minister of Education for Northern Ireland from 1921 to 1926, who, in September 1921, set up the Lynn Commission to consider educational reform. Miss Matier was a member of this committee, which was headed by Robert Lynn, editor of the *Northern Whig*, and comprised over thirty members. The 1923 Act (also known as the Londonderry Act)

Tennis party at Drumglass, *c.*1930

was chiefly concerned with implementing an integrated system of education and addressing religious instruction in primary schools, but there were also changes to the financing and management of secondary schools, which would now be assisted by local government and subject to certain demands. Higher fees were now paid to schools for each pupil over eleven who had passed an entrance examination and for those who had passed the Junior Certificate, which replaced the Intermediate Board examinations in 1925. The government increased its contribution to teachers' salaries and a statutory pension scheme was begun. In return for this aid, schools agreed to inspection by the Ministry of Education, to come under a recognised board of governors which would liaise with the Ministry, and to enter pupils for the public examinations.

The political and educational changes in Northern Ireland were marked at the school's annual prize distributions, for Miss Matier, like Dr Byers before her, realised the importance of securing support from influential circles and bringing to their attention the school's traditions and achievements. Thus, in 1921, Lady Craig, wife of Sir James Craig, the first Prime Minister of Northern Ireland, distributed the prizes, and the platform party included the parliamentary secretary to the Ministry of Education. In 1924 Lady Londonderry, wife of the Minister of Education, was the guest of honour at the prize distribution. On this occasion Miss Matier evoked Victoria College's long and successful history and its pioneering work in the education of girls. She remarked that from its origins in 1859 the school had turned out 'distinguished women as well as fine scholars', who were to be found in every part of the British Empire 'as educationalists, social workers or homemakers'.[35]

INTERNAL DEVELOPMENTS

In the midst of political and educational changes, Victoria College continued to expand. A Girl Guide company, 71st Belfast, was formed in 1924, and the prefect system was introduced.

Another important development was school dinners for day girls. Miss Matier was concerned that pupils should have the opportunity to enjoy a hot meal at midday and duly engaged Miss Newett as cook. Miss Newett had worked in a munitions factory during the war and was another strong character who ran her 'little empire' with great efficiency until her retirement in 1945. The kitchen was a hive of industry and Miss Newett had little time for anyone who 'shilly-shallied', or for any girl who forgot to put her name in the pillar box before 10 a.m. if she wished to have a meal that day.[36]

Victoria College continued to offer girls a wide and varied education and expanded its curriculum to meet new demands. Pupils were prepared for the Junior and Senior Leaving Certificates organised by the Ministry of Education, and also for the matriculation examinations of Queen's University Belfast, Trinity College Dublin and the University of London, and the Oxford and Cambridge entrance examinations. Those not wishing to continue to tertiary education might take courses in modern literature or domestic science, where they learned 'high-class, plain and invalid cookery', as well as dressmaking, laundry-work and hygiene. They could also enter the secretarial department, which taught English, typewriting, shorthand, bookkeeping, business training, invoicing, filing, duplicating and precis writing.[37]

The pupils enjoyed a breadth of learning with an emphasis on art and music. Art classes were held in large airy rooms and girls were taught object, imaginative and geometrical drawing. Classes in applied art were wide-ranging and included leatherwork, stencilling and embroidery. Private tuition was offered in violin, piano and singing, and there was an opportunity to enter examinations run by the Associated Board of the Royal Academy of Music and the Royal College of Music.

In 1891 the National Froebel Union began to train and examine kindergarten teachers. Dr Byers had started a teacher training course at Victoria College to raise the level of teaching in Ulster and, consequently, the standard of education, but also to ensure that she had a pool of quality teachers. The first of her students received their certificates in 1904.[38] In 1928 the National Froebel Union gave recognition to its colleges in the United Kingdom and, following rigorous tests, Victoria was officially approved by the Union. It was the only school in Northern Ireland to receive this endorsement and continued to offer training for kindergarten teachers until 1956.

EXPANSION: DRUMGLASS HOUSE AND STRATHEARN JUNIOR SCHOOL

To your initiative and enterprise is largely due the expansion of Victoria College – in the foundation of a Hall of Residence at Drumglass House, and the establishment of a Junior School at Strathearn.
ADDRESS BY FORMER PUPILS AND STAFF TO MISS MATIER[39]

Numbers at Victoria continued to rise in the post-war years. This placed tremendous pressure on the school, which struggled to accommodate all the pupils, and a number of applicants was turned away. When Dr Byers had been faced with a similar situation in 1887, she had moved the younger children out of Lower Crescent; it was now decided to relocate the boarding department and turn the dormitories into much needed classrooms. A new house of residence was thus required. Miss Matier had strong views as to what was needed and what would be 'a worthy helpmate' to Victoria College. She herself had been a resident pupil at the school and believed that the boarders should grow up in fine surroundings, with trees and grass where they could expend their energies; she wanted them to have the amenities of the country in the town. When Sir Henry Musgrave's house at Drumglass, south Belfast, became available in 1922, it seemed perfect, and Miss Matier encouraged the board of governors to purchase it.[40]

Drumglass House was duly acquired. Mary Rogers, a pupil in the 1920s, explained that her mother had visited Drumglass with Miss Matier as a prospective buyer, and she persuaded the headmistress to buy most of the drawing-room furniture to make the boarders feel more comfortable in their new home. Drumglass House was remodelled under Miss Matier's direction – a sun parlour, dormitories and cloakrooms were added to the house, while tennis courts and playing fields were made in the grounds; the Dutch garden was retained and well tended.[41] In her annual school report for 1922 Miss Matier declared with pride that now, for the first time, Victoria was to have 'a residence worthy of the ambitions of its lovers and its own record'.[42]

In 1926 there were plans to build a two-storey house 'of artistic appearance' within the grounds for the headmistress' residence. A budget of £1,800 was set and the cost was to be defrayed by the sale of 2 Lower Crescent. The following year the house was ready for occupation and inspected by several members of the board of governors. Miss Cunningham, principal from 1951 to 1976, later remarked on the spaciousness of the residence, particularly for one person, and claimed she 'rattled around it like a pea'.[43] Drumglass House was an ideal home for any pupil. Other later additions included Vita Glass Hall, which opened in 1928 for the kindergarten, and Drumglass Hall, opened in 1935 for prize days and functions. Vita Glass was named after the special ultraviolet-light transmitting glass with which it was glazed; this was highly fashionable at the time and thought to be therapeutic.

Drumglass House officially opened as a boarders' residence in September 1923. It was advertised as being located in one of the healthiest suburbs of Belfast and surrounded by gardens and playing fields for hockey, tennis, lacrosse and cricket. There were plans to open a school for gardening to train students in horticulture and prepare them for the Diploma of the Royal Horticultural Society; Miss Matier was herself a lover of gardens.[44] The first annual prize distribution was held at Drumglass House in June 1924. Lady Londonderry was invited as the guest of honour and distributed the prizes in a marquee in the grounds. Miss Matier's speech was both witty and eloquent. She described the occasion as 'a housewarming' and 'a sort of entry into the Promised Land', for although they had purchased the building two years earlier and had hoped to have access to it prior to this, she had forgotten 'the Canaanites, Hittites and the Jebusites, namely the plumbers, bricklayers and plasterers'. These obstacles and other obstructions, such as paint pots in the hall, had postponed the 'state entry'.[45]

Five years later Victoria College expanded across Belfast and opened a junior school at Strathearn House, Belmont. The initiative for this venture came from parents living in east Belfast, who asked the board of governors to open a branch on their side of town. The board secured a loan from the Ulster Bank and Strathearn House was purchased. At fourteen years

The Dutch garden at Drumglass

A garden party at Drumglass House, 1930

Strathearn House

Strathearn School

In the early days Victoria made considerable
financial sacrifices so that the younger school
might be adequately housed and equipped, and
several long-cherished plans of her own had to be
postponed; but more valuable even than financial
aid, Victoria gave to Strathearn the support of
her own good name and reputation, and for
guidance her own high standards of scholarship
and achievement.

VICTORIA COLLEGE BELFAST CENTENARY 1859–1959[47]

The success of Victoria College prompted parents
living in the Belmont and Knock areas of Belfast to
request that the board of governors consider opening
a branch school in east Belfast. Miss Matier was
very keen to expand and at her instigation the board
acquired Strathearn House, Belmont, a splendid
nineteenth-century building set in eighteen acres of
grounds. There were tennis courts, a large pond and
porters' lodges, which were later occupied by the staff.
The conservatory was subsequently knocked down to
make room for an assembly hall.

Had the board of governors established
Strathearn as a separate school, or even as an affiliated
school, it would have been eligible for a Head's grant
from the Ministry of Education for Northern Ireland.
This would have considerably reduced the cost of the
venture to Victoria College. However, Miss Matier and
Mr Pollock, the chair of the board, were adamant that
the new school should be a part of Victoria College
and remain under its control. They therefore decided
to forego the Ministry's grant and secure a loan from
the Ulster Bank to purchase Strathearn House.[47] As
Brenda Berner (née Kenyon) explained:

> The erstwhile daughter had become the
> younger sister and everyone at Strathearn
> was united in their effort and desire to prove
> worthy of the freedom and be at least
> the equal of Victoria in academic and
> sporting achievements.[48]

In 1929 Strathearn Junior School opened
with sixty-three pupils and was staffed by teachers
from Lower Crescent, who were 'enthusiastic and

committed'.[49] Although Miss Matier, as principal of Victoria College, had responsibility for the school, it was run by Miss Miskelly, who had previously taught Classics at Victoria. The school welcomed boys and girls from the age of four; boys left when they were eight, while girls continued until fourteen and then transferred to the main school at Lower Crescent to complete their education. Pupils wore the Victoria College uniform, but the ribbon on their hat bore the letters SJS, not VCB.

The new school was an undoubted success. On the eve of the Second World War numbers at Strathearn had doubled. However, attendance was affected badly by the air raids, for Strathearn was in a vulnerable location between Stormont and the shipyards; indeed, two bombs landed on the school's hockey field. Pupils were initially evacuated to the Argory, near Dungannon, but subsequently joined the Victoria girls at Portballintrae. For those who remained at Strathearn, school life was put on a war footing. The girls 'Dug for Victory' in the former fruit garden, which was made into a vegetable patch, and air raid shelters were built in the grounds.

By the end of the war, numbers had risen and there were two hundred pupils on the register. By this time Miss Adelaide Rodden had taken over as headmistress (1944–58). As one former pupil recalled, 'her fearsome reputation preceded her', but she was a dedicated and encouraging teacher who kept in touch with girls after they had left.[50]

The junior school gradually sought independence. Following Miss Matier's resignation as principal of Drumglass and Strathearn in 1936, it was agreed that the headmistress of Victoria College should now act as an advisor, consultant and visitor, and liaise with the board of governors on Strathearn's behalf. The principals of the two branch schools (Drumglass and Strathearn) were, however, expected 'to maintain the traditions of Victoria College and inculcate loyalty and attachment to the parent college'.[51]

In 1949 ties were further loosened when a separate board of governors was established for Strathearn. This comprised eight members and was formally called the Strathearn Committee of the Victoria College Board of Governors to reflect its affiliation to the founding school. A new uniform was introduced to mark Strathearn's growing independence. The girls now wore a green tunic and a fawn shirt and socks, but the tie and scarf bore a maroon stripe as an acknowledgement of the school's link with Victoria.

There were additional changes in the fifties, when it was decided to convert Strathearn into a senior school so that pupils might complete their education there. Extra classroom space was required and a building programme begun, and in 1955 Strathearn was established as a fully-fledged senior school.

In 1988 Strathearn sought to sever its ties completely with the parent school. The board of governors of Victoria College subsequently relinquished control and granted ownership of the school to the Strathearn Committee, which duly established its own board of governors. Strathearn was now recognised as a school independent from Victoria.[52]

Prize-giving at Strathearn, December 1945. Brenda Kenyon, head girl, is presented to Mrs J.C. McDermott; also in the photograph are (L–R) Professor Gilbert Waterhouse (governor), Miss Adelaide Rodden (head of Strathearn) and Mrs Grace Faris (headmistress of Victoria College).

Nineteenth-century stained glass window, Drumglass House

of age pupils from Strathearn transferred to the main school to complete their secondary education, but as Brenda Berner (née Kenyon) recalls, they never felt like new girls.

Despite the desolation of the post-war years, Victoria College grew and expanded from one school into three, with branches at Drumglass House and Strathearn. This development was largely due to Miss Matier and her vision for the future. Drumglass and Strathearn were very much 'her creations' and it was fitting that upon her retirement as headmistress of Victoria College, she was presented with an illuminated address with illustrations of Victoria College, Drumglass House, the headmistress' house and Strathearn, as well as views of Cave Hill.

THE END OF A REGENCY

When I look back on past days I feel that I can say like a famous teacher of
old, 'I have learned much from my masters, more from my fellow-teachers,
but most of all from my pupils', and it is for the enriching of a lifetime […]
that I thank you from my heart.
ANNA MATIER[53]

In 1930 Miss Matier resigned as headmistress of Victoria College after a lifetime's service to the school – she spent eighteen years as headmistress, four years as vice principal and many more as a pupil and member of staff. The occasion was marked by presentations from the Old Girls' Association (OGA) and the staff; Mr George Smith, the music teacher, composed a poem in her honour. A presentation was also made by the Ulster Headmistresses' Association, of which Miss Matier had been president for several years, aided by her secretaries, Miss Shearman (of Ashleigh House School) and Miss Purvis (of Richmond Lodge School).

Miss Matier had sought to retire from the headship of Victoria College prior to this, and in 1923 she offered the post to her former pupil, Helen Waddell – the remuneration was £400 per annum and rooms at the newly acquired Drumglass House. This was a time of great change for Northern Ireland and its education system and these developments may have prompted Miss Matier to seek a younger successor. Helen, who was thirty-three years old at the time and actively seeking a lectureship, was not, however, tempted by the administrative responsibilities of the job and was heavily dissuaded from accepting the post by the academics at Bedford College in the University of London. She explained this to her sister, Meg, in May 1923:

> I can't bring myself to do it […] It's only the thought of not being the
> usual 'Irish absentee' that goads me. I've spoken to my blessed
> 'Spurgeon' and Miss Tuke, and they both say it's almost 'criminal'
> to go and bury myself alive in administration. […] I'd do it if I
> was sure it was my duty but I can't see it.[54]

Miss Matier thus continued in office, perhaps awaiting a suitable successor, whom she found in Mrs Grace Faris, who rejoined the teaching staff following the death of her husband in 1925. In 1930 Miss Matier suggested to the board of governors that they appoint Mrs Faris to succeed her. Mrs Faris duly took over as headmistress of Victoria College, although Miss

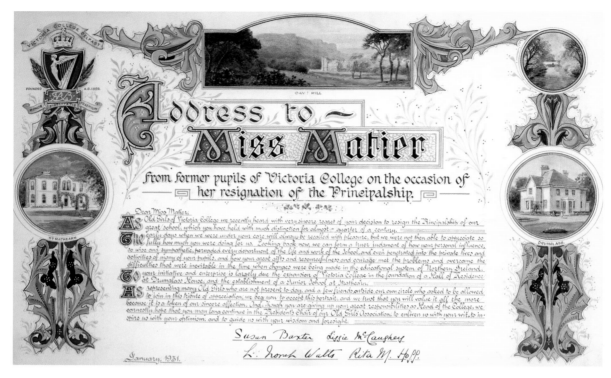

Illuminated address presented to Miss Matier by former pupils
upon her retirement, January 1931

Victoria College and Drumglass House

The unveiling of Gerald Festus Kelly's portrait of Miss Matier (second from the right) at the Carlton Hall, 3 January 1931. Mrs Grace Faris, headmistress, stands to the right of the portrait; the Rt Hon. H.M. Pollock, chair of the board of governors, is on the far right.

Matier continued to act as principal of the two branch schools at Drumglass and Strathearn, and to live in the headmistress' house within the grounds of Drumglass until her death in 1944. For several years she remained on the board of governors and was a pivotal member of the OGA, often hosting reunions and entertaining members with her repartee and lavish hospitality. Miss Matier also entertained the senior girls. Kathleen Davey (née Burrows) remembered vividly how, as one of four House captains, she was invited to Miss Matier's for afternoon tea. Kathleen was presented with a choice of four mouth-watering cakes and when asked by her hostess which she would like, politely replied that she did not mind. This elicited the tart retort, 'If you cannot make your mind up about a piece of cake, Kathleen, you will never make up your mind.' Some seventy years later Kathleen reflected on how many rash decisions she had made as a consequence of 'this challenge'.[55]

In 1936 Miss Matier relinquished all of her duties; old age and increasing infirmity were taking their toll. Following an accident, she was confined to her room and she continued to physically and mentally decline until her death in June 1944. Former pupils and colleagues paid tribute to their benevolent tyrant by publishing a collection of tributes in her memory as a supplement to the 1945 edition of *The Victorian*. As one contributor noted:

> She ruled as an autocrat her little world, the world of the school.
> It was a rule that might not suit the modern generation of schoolgirls –
> I only know that it suited us and we were her devoted subjects.[56]

4

'The vanguard of progress'

The Faris Years, 1930–51

She lived in no ivory tower; she was a woman
of action, an assiduous organiser, an unwearied
promoter of schemes for perfecting school routine.

ROSE McLERNON[1]

Mrs Grace Faris, portrait by T.C. Dugdale, 1952

In 1930 the board of governors appointed Mrs Grace Faris (née Acheson) to succeed Miss Matier as headmistress of Victoria College. Mrs Faris led the school for twenty-one years but gave a lifetime's service to Victoria, first as a pupil and student of Dr Byers (she was one of the last to graduate from the collegiate department), thereafter as a teacher and headmistress, and finally as a member of the board of governors and president of the Old Girls' Association (OGA). Mrs Faris entered Victoria College as a pupil in 1900. She taught part-time at the school while completing her MA at Queen's University Belfast and was then a full-time member of staff until her marriage to the Reverend George Faris in 1912. Following her husband's death in 1925, Mrs Faris returned to teaching, and from then until her retirement in 1951 'was at the throbbing heart of the school's dramatic expansion'.[2] Mrs Faris' family association to Victoria began in the early days of the school and continues today. Mrs Faris' mother, Harriet Glasgow, and her aunts, sisters, daughters and granddaughter were pupils and teachers at the school. Her son, Professor John Faris, was for many years a member of the board of governors, of which he was chairman from 1976 to 1985.

Like her predecessors, Mrs Faris played a prominent role in educational reforms and especially in the promotion of women in the profession. She sat on committees for the Ministry of Education and the Association of Headmistresses' and in 1932 was elected president of the Queen's Women's Graduate Association. Mrs Faris was a co-opted member of the Queen's University senate from 1936 and in 1949 was nominated as a member by King George VI, replacing the Countess of Clanwilliam. In total, she was a member of the senate for twenty-three years. Mrs Faris' contribution to education was acknowledged in 1948 when she was awarded the MBE.

THE INTER-WAR YEARS: ACQUISITION AND EXPANSION

Victoria College, by the vision and foresight of its headmistresses,
was in the vanguard of progress.
VICTORIA COLLEGE BELFAST CENTENARY, 1859–1959[3]

Mrs Faris steered the school through difficult and challenging times. She was confronted with a world war, revolutionary changes in education and the birth of the voluntary grammar school. Yet she sustained Victoria College's reputation for academic excellence, and preserved its tradition of providing a liberal education and a foundation for good citizenship. Mrs Faris built on her predecessors' legacy and, like them, was concerned to progress the school in accordance with changing demands. One of her first projects was the school library. There had once been a well-stocked library, but when the collegiate department was closed in the early twentieth century, the collections were scattered. Mrs Faris made it her priority to revive and revamp the library. She secured a grant from the government and donations from the OGA, and appointed Miss Turkington ('Turkie') as the first librarian. The books were duly organised and given their distinctive red linen covers. In 1940 a junior library was also established with the help of a government subsidy.

Another early development was the introduction of the House system in March 1936. This was initiated by several of the school prefects and was intended to encourage competition on the sports field and to foster camaraderie among girls of different ages. There were four Houses, each with their own distinctive colour – North (yellow or orange), South (blue), East (purple) and Country (green). They were seemingly named after the school's catchment areas, but girls were allocated to the Houses indiscriminately, a cause of great excitement and anticipation. Each House was run by a captain chosen by the headmistress and staff; a games captain and three committee members were elected by the girls. Every pupil wore a badge in her House colour and attended House meetings. From 1927 the House captains contributed short reports to the school magazine, *The Victorian*. In 1939 competition between Houses was heightened with the introduction of a conduct award. Girls who were late or misbehaved were issued with an order mark against their House. The Houses were involved in charity work and during the war raised money to help the Forces by organising concerts, beetle drives, treasure hunts and even a funfair complete with a chamber of horrors and fortune teller. In 1942 North House organised a Christmas market that raised £22 5s 6d for Mrs Churchill's Aid to Russia Fund, the Red Cross and the Comfort Fund.[4] When the school moved from Lower Crescent in 1972, the Houses were renamed to reflect the four sites Victoria College has occupied since its foundation – Wellington (yellow), Howard (blue), Pakenham (purple) and Crescent (green). After Victoria's amalgamation with Richmond Lodge School in 1987, two additional Houses were formed to mark this development in the school's history – Marlborough (red) and Richmond (white).

During the inter-war years the girls continued to work hard and play hard. Alongside their academic work they enjoyed a variety of sports including cricket, badminton, swimming, drill and gymnastics. Hockey and tennis remained the favourites, and the annual staff–pupil hockey match was a highlight of the school year. An attempt to introduce lacrosse in 1932 met with a tepid response. Few turned out to practices and attempts to rally support fell on deaf ears; the game was abandoned soon after.

The school continued to expand and faced the perennial problem of space. The board of governors made several acquisitions to try and accommodate the extra pupils. In 1934, 1 Lower Crescent was bought for the preparatory department and the rooms formerly occupied by the younger children were converted into classrooms. While the preparatory department was now separate – 'down the Crescent' – all the pupils came together for morning assembly at 9 a.m., when rows of chattering girls were silenced by the whistle of the gym mistress.[5]

The main event in Mrs Faris' headship prior to the outbreak of the Second World War was the opening of Drumglass Hall in 1935, the year of George V's silver jubilee. The new hall could accommodate eight hundred people and was to be used for concerts and school functions. The official opening was on 18 January 1935 and it was combined with the annual prize distribution. The ceremony was performed by Mrs Neville Chamberlain, wife of the chancellor of the exchequer, who also attended. Mrs Chamberlain was presented with a golden key with which to open the building formally and was later given a silver casket containing Irish linen handkerchiefs embroidered with her monogram. A number of distinguished guests was present including Lord Craigavon, the first prime minister of Northern Ireland, and the Right Honourable H.M. Pollock, Minister of Finance for Northern Ireland and chairman of the school's board of governors.

The inter-war years were otherwise a period of consolidation and progress; the traditions of the school were preserved while changes were continually made to meet new demands. The daily routine was punctured by affairs of national importance, such as the death of George V in 1936. Kathleen Davey (née Burrows), who was a resident pupil at the time, recalled how news of the king's imminent death, overheard on a staff wireless, elicited from her a 'crazy reaction'. She secreted some official school writing paper, sent a letter of condolence to Queen Mary and received a letter of thanks in reply.[6] Representatives from the school attended the Coronation Youth Rally in London on 18 May 1937, where they joined some ten thousand young people from across the British Empire for the opening ceremony in the Royal Albert Hall and a service in Westminster Abbey.

For many at Victoria College, 1937 was remembered for the fire that broke out in January – 'the one really exciting event of this term'. It was caused by a defect in the heating system. Ambulances, a fire engine and a dozen hefty firemen duly arrived on the scene, but there was no serious danger and the blaze was soon controlled. The girls were given a half-day holiday and the school was without heating for several days. However, a burst of drill for ten minutes at the start of each lesson kept the winter chill at bay.[7]

VICTORIA DURING THE SECOND WORLD WAR

While the 'anvils and hammers of the shop of war are working to fashion out
the instruments of armed justice in defence of beleaguered truth' there must
still be 'pens and heads there sitting by their studious lamps, musing, searching,
recording new notions and ideas'.

GRACE FARIS[8]

In September 1939 Britain was once again at war but this time – and for the first time – the safety of the school was threatened. Mrs Faris' annual reports offer a vivid insight into the impact of war on the daily life of the school. At first there was little real effect, although there were outward manifestations of war, such as gasmasks sitting on the desks alongside books and the air-raid drills that were undertaken in complete silence. The girls would congregate for a quick roll call in shelters in Crescent Gardens, where the science block was later built.[9] There were also preparations for evacuation, but it was not until November 1939 that this seemed likely to happen; initially evacuation was but 'a chimera'.[10] War efforts were soon intensified. The older girls attended Civil Defence lectures where they learnt how to use the stirrup pump against incendiaries and to crawl to safety out of a smoke-filled room. Prefects ran lectures in first aid and home nursing and certificates were awarded by the St John Ambulance. Miss Norah Clarke, head of the science department, led an incendiary disposal squad of senior girls.[11] Fuel was in short supply and heating was provided by open turf fires. Florence Allen (née Hamilton) recalls that it was her task as the class prefect to choose a helpmate and fill a bucket with turf from the yard. On one occasion a teacher lost a ring in the stack but, eventually, as the pile was depleted, Florence managed to retrieve the precious object, a great coup.[12]

Victoria College during the war – note
the gas masks on the desks, *c*.1940

The Evacuation School at Portballintrae: August 1940–June 1945

The evacuation school at Portballintrae will rank as one of the most interesting and successful experiments in the history of the school.
GRACE FARIS[13]

In 1940 Drumglass House was requisitioned by the government, and the boarders, along with some of the day girls, were evacuated to the North Antrim coast. The group first stayed at Glenarm Castle with Mrs Faris and her three children, Katherine, Sandy and John. Mary Balfour (née Lindsay) remembers the coldness of Glenarm during their three-week stay, and also the daily dose of tomato juice for good health.[14] Glenarm Castle was also subsequently commandeered by the Ministry and the group had to relocate to Portballintrae. In early autumn 1940 the Evacuation School was opened at the Red House Hotel (later the Beach Hotel, and now flats) and the nearby Alt-na-Craig House; houses which, as Mrs

Faris explained, 'defy the wild gales of the Antrim Coast and offer a warm welcome to those who have been battling them'.[15]

For five years a mini-Victoria College functioned on the North Antrim coast, first under Miss Agnes Wasson, who had replaced Miss Matier as warden of Drumglass, then under Miss Adelaide Rodden and, finally, under Miss Hogg. Matron Rose Heaney took care of any sickness but was also in charge of the tuck cupboard on the landing and issued goodies once a day. Miss Glasgow, the housekeeper at Drumglass, was responsible for planning and cooking the meals and, despite the rationing, managed to provide 'interesting and wholesome' food for the ever-increasing number of girls. She allegedly boosted supplies with food washed ashore from wrecks.[16]

The Red House Hotel and Alt-na-Craig were modified to accommodate a school and a boarding department, which were run by a skeleton staff of teachers from Lower Crescent. One mistress from each department 'voluntarily went into exile' and those who remained in Belfast relieved their colleagues during the school holidays. Staffing shortages and a

The Portballintrae Evacuation School, 1944

lack of facilities were overcome through associations with other schools, chiefly the Richmond Lodge Evacuation School, which was located at the Bayhead Hotel, Portballintrae, and was run by Miss Wilson. The government 'heartily approved' of the two schools' proposal to combine classes and Miss Wilson later recalled that this had proven to be a most successful and mutually beneficial arrangement, as well as 'a friendly and pleasant association'. The two schools remained separate and each had its own assembly, but pupils came together for a number of lessons and shared teachers; accordingly they managed to cover all of the subjects on the curriculum. Senior classes were generally held in the Red House, while the juniors had their lessons in the Bayhead.[17] This union was a foreshadowing of the amalgamation in 1987.

Daily life in Portballintrae

School life, like every other, is made up not of grand occasions but mostly of ordinary everyday expressions and in it we learn more and more the importance of the unimportant. It teaches us to derive pleasure and profit in small things whether they be, as in our case, salvaging on the beach, wood gathering or berry picking; yet there co-exists the tendency when we are far removed from city life to become detached and engrossed in school routine and to lose our awareness that we are living in the presence of history. Let us never forget that 'ages hence shall this our lofty scene be acted o'er in states unborn and accents yet unknown'.

AGNES WASSON[18]

Miss Wasson established a family community at Portballintrae and former pupils remember this as a very happy and even idyllic time, albeit rather cold. Ann Cumming, who was only eight when she joined the Evacuation School in 1941, recalls the coldness indoors and the wind outside; others remember the frost traceries that formed on the inside of the windows during winter. The houses were heated by open turf fires on which the girls roasted potatoes and made smoky toast during break. According to Romayne Carswell (née Ferris), there was scarcely a ruler that was not scorched at both ends 'from doing duty as a toasting fork'.[19]

The girls had much greater freedom in Portballintrae than in the city. There were walks in the dunes, swimming in the sea and rounders on the beach, regardless of the weather. A gymnasium was set up in the garage of the Red House Hotel and hockey was played twice a week on the pitch belonging to Bushmills Secondary School; this school also gave the girls access to their tennis courts. The Richmond Lodge evacuees allowed the Victoria girls to use their netball field. On Sundays the girls walked to Bushmills and back for church, a distance of several miles; otherwise there were dance classes, picnics, films and talks at weekends. For a special treat they were taken to Barry's Amusements in Portrush.[20] Miss Wasson was concerned that in such glorious surroundings they would all forget the momentousness of what was happening in the world. The girls were thus encouraged to help with the war effort and started a War Savings group. They knitted garments for the wool depot and raised money for the Forces. The proceeds from one fancy dress party went to the Spitfire Fund, while a carnival was held in aid of the Air Raid Distress Fund.

Although the surroundings at Portballintrae were very different from those of Lower Crescent, the basic structure of school life was preserved. The girls progressed with their lessons and sat public examinations. Mary Balfour (née Lindsay), whose grandmother owned Alt-na-Craig House, remembers taking her Junior Certificate in one of the ground-floor rooms and seeing a naval incident on the horizon. Even science classes continued for the facilities at Bushmills Secondary School were made available to the Evacuation School. An annual prize distribution was held in the dining room of the Red House Hotel, and each year Mrs Norah Watts, who was on the board of governors, would visit the school to give out the prizes. There were sports days, galas and concerts. Anyone who wished could take music lessons with

Miss Bell, who always had a large jigsaw 'on hand' to occupy the large number of girls who arrived at her bungalow too early for their lessons.[21] A special evacuation Girl Guide company was set up and most of the pupils joined either the Brownies or Guides, where they worked for badges and contributed to the war effort. The Evacuation School had its own prefects and introduced the House system to liven up competition on sports days. All the pupils, including the Richmond Lodge evacuees, were divided into three Houses: Dunluce, Rathlin and Moyle.

The Evacuation School was strongly modelled on Victoria College and relied on the help and support it received from the Belfast school. Miss Wasson emphasised this link and paid tribute to the tremendous support they had received from Mrs Faris and her staff:

> Many of our ways are reminiscent of
> Victoria College Belfast – in fact,
> as far as possible that is so – though in

such dissimilar circumstances there are bound to be increasing differences. But looking back after one and a half years here we value above all else – for they have been an anchorage while many things have changed or passed – the traditions of Victoria College Belfast and the leadership of Mrs Faris, whose faith and counsel and encouragement have been our strength.[22]

Mrs Faris was a regular visitor to Portballintrae. She was determined to maintain links between the two schools and ensure that these girls felt part of Victoria College. Former pupils remember how their headmistress would visit most weekends, a tremendous achievement given her many other responsibilities. The girls greatly looked forward to Mrs Faris' arrival and her visits to the junior dormitory to kiss the little ones goodnight.[23] Dr McLernon also made a weekly journey to the Evacuation School. She came to teach

Cycling on the beach at Portballintrae

the girls German, but invariably brought with her packages and messages from the Belfast pupils. The evacuees received books for their library from Lower Crescent twice a term, but perhaps the most important link with the Belfast school – at least, as far as the girls were concerned – was the St Patrick's Day hockey match between Victoria College and the Portballintrae Evacuation School. The Belfast team would travel up north for the match, providing an opportunity for old friends to catch up and exchange news.

Astrid Maddocks (née McMath) joined the Evacuation School in April 1945. She had been evacuated from London since her education there was badly affected by the air raids – Astrid and her fellow pupils had spent more time in the shelters than in the classroom. When Astrid's parents suggested that she might go to boarding school, she eagerly accepted and was not disappointed. Astrid thoroughly enjoyed her brief time at Portballintrae and the general contentment of life there. She recalls the warm welcome she received from the girls, who immediately gave her a nickname and later sent her sweets and comics when she was confined to the sanatorium with German measles.[24]

Many of the evacuees recall the VE Day celebrations, which marked the end of the war and, consequently, their stay in Portballintrae. There was a picnic in the sandhills 'with some disappointingly scorched stew at lunch', but the highlight was an invitation from Campbell College Evacuation School to join its celebratory dance in Portrush and enjoy a wonderful bonfire on the beach.[25]

Most of the boarders who were evacuated to Portballintrae in 1940 completed their education there and did not return as pupils to Lower Crescent. Conversely, those who arrived back in Belfast after the war and represented the boarders' homecoming had never before set foot in Victoria College or in Drumglass House. Many were filled with apprehension and sadness when they boarded the bus at Portrush in June 1945, knowing that they would not be returning there the following September. Swimming in the Ormeau Baths and the afternoon croc were

Exploring the rock pools at Portballintrae

poor substitutes for the dunes and the sea, while the high trees around Drumglass seemed confining after the open expanse of the coast. Moreover, the maze of corridors and the sea of alien faces in Lower Crescent were quite bewildering for the newcomers, who watched cliques of girls eating sandwiches and preparing for classes. However, Drumglass House soon became home. An influx of painters, plumbers and workmen started renovations, the trees were appreciated for their climbing – until 'tops of trees' were declared out of bounds – and friends were made. The unfamiliar became familiar and the evacuees were glad to be part of the school rather than an adjunct. Mrs Faris welcomed the return of the boarders, which marked a return to normality, and the editor of *The Victorian* pronounced this 'the main event of the year'. But, for Romayne Carswell, 'school was never as remarkable again'.[26]

The life of a school is, as a general rule, little affected by events in the outside world. But the world war has shaken the most stable institutions out of their grooves and Victoria College, like other schools, has suffered a war change.

GRACE FARIS[27]

Every pupil was involved with collecting and salvaging materials, particularly those who were members of the school Guide company. Audrey Graham (née Alexander) remembered trundling along the Stranmillis Road with her handcart collecting scrap paper for the Paper Control Board. The Guides helped at rest centres and first-aid posts after air raids, and they made camouflage nets. However, all Guide camps were postponed during the war years as sleeping under canvas would make them 'a military objective'. The Victoria girls collected books for the salvage men and in March 1943 managed to fill nine large bags. The men revealed that the most bags any school had managed to fill was nine and a half, but claimed that these had been much lighter than Victoria's sacks; Dr Byers' insistence on heavy duty reading had evidently been honoured by her successors. Pupils were warned to be thrifty and conserve resources. According to Joan Ardill (née Buchanan), all jotters were carefully inspected before a new one was issued.[28] A War Savings group was started and the girls were encouraged to put aside a little money each week to help with the war effort. They were also urged to knit for victory and support the Wool Depot, which was run by several militant members of the OGA who struggled to generate enthusiasm. The annual report for the Wool Depot in 1943 reported that all requests for new knitters had seemingly fallen on deaf ears. Nevertheless, by the end of the war the girls and former pupils had managed to knit nine hundred articles for the Forces – including forty-eight pairs of mittens and socks for the Old Boys from Campbell College Belfast (the Old Campbellians).[29]

A constant reminder of the war was the barrage balloon stationed in Lower Crescent. Every time this ascended, girls in the classrooms overlooking the Crescent would flock to the windows, much to the chagrin of their teachers. Mary Balfour (née Lindsay) arrived at Victoria College from England in September 1939 and clearly remembers how they would hear the soldiers singing popular songs from their quarters in the Crescent Church hall.[30]

Perhaps the most significant consequence of the war was the requisitioning of Drumglass House by the government and the subsequent evacuation of the boarding department to Portballintrae (see pp. 84–7). During the war Drumglass was used as a censorship office – all mail coming into and leaving Northern Ireland was checked there for any suspicious content. With the government occupying Drumglass, the boarders, under their warden Miss Wasson, set up an evacuation school at Portballintrae and were joined by some of the day girls and pupils from Strathearn; about a third of the school relocated to the North Antrim coast. Thus, from August 1940 until June 1945, Victoria College was split and two parallel schools operated in tandem. But, as Mrs Faris explained, without the boarders, the school was not itself.

Despite the anxiety and upheaval of the war, school life continued. Indeed, it was essential that there was a sense of normality, routine and structure; as Audrey Graham recalled:

The business of teaching and learning was the first essential and this gave a sense of purpose to years which might otherwise have been filled with confusion.[31]

Thelma Hopkins, 1955

Examinations were taken and Victoria College sustained its reputation for academic excellence. There were annual fixtures, such as the end of year concert in June, which marked 'the end of classroom bondage and the beginning of summer freedom'.[32] The requisitioning of Drumglass meant that prize distributions were temporarily held in the lecture hall at Lower Crescent, and given the lack of space, they were attended only by staff and pupils – 'somewhat of a war substitute'. For the last two years of the war, however, prize day was made a public affair once more as, thanks to Great Victoria Street Presbyterian Church, the school had use of Smyth Hall.[33]

Societies continued to meet during the war, although the German Circle was suspended. The sporting life of the school continued and Victoria teams achieved considerable success in inter-school competitions. The tennis team won the first ever Ulster Schools' Tennis Cup in 1939, while the hockey team won both the Senior League and the Ulster Women's Charity Cup in 1942, establishing Victoria's as the premier team in Ulster. It was at this time that Thelma Hopkins, a pupil who would go on to become one of Ulster's most successful sportswomen, joined the school. Thelma entered Victoria College in 1943, aged seven, and she still recalls the 'trauma' of her first arithmetic lesson. She represented Northern Ireland in both squash and hockey and distinguished herself in a number of track and field events. In 1954, when still a pupil at Victoria, Thelma was a double medal winner at the Commonwealth Games in Vancouver, taking gold in the high jump and silver in the long jump; the same year she won the high jump at the European Championships in Berne. In 1955 Thelma was named Britain's Woman Athlete of the Year, but 1956 was the pinnacle of her career, for she broke the world high-jump record and took silver at the Olympic Games in Melbourne. Thelma now lives in Canada but recalls, with fondness, the support she was given by her teachers, who always impressed upon her the importance of having a solid education, but backed her sporting endeavours and ensured she was never late for those all important practices at Bladon Drive.[34]

During the war, the number of pupils at Victoria College continued to increase and, in fact, reached an all time high. Mrs Faris wondered how the school would manage to accommodate all the girls when the evacuees returned. Additional buildings were secured to provide extra classroom space. A house in the Crescent that adjoined the school was converted into a physics laboratory, while 9 Lower Crescent was bought to accommodate the new canteen, which was one of the first in Northern Ireland. Victoria College now joined the School Meals Scheme, recently introduced by the Ministry of Education, and served two hundred dinners each day. Pupils were instructed to walk, not run, down the Crescent to the canteen in their customary croc, but invariably ignored the warning and, as Moira McKelvey (née Hopkins) recalls, once free of the school building they would sprint. The new canteen was under the management of Miss Glasgow, who had previously cooked for the Evacuation School in Portballintrae. She remained in charge until her retirement in 1969 and ensured that the girls always had good food, even when there was rationing. Brenda Berner (née Kenyon) explains that while Miss Glasgow's 'kind heart was kept firmly hidden', it was discovered by girls sitting their Senior Certificate, who would find an extra treat after dessert to fortify them for the afternoon's examinations – perhaps a piece of cake or the 'ultimate luxury', a chocolate marshmallow.[35] The girls sat at tables of eight or ten and, according to Joyce Moran (née Weatherup), they were expected to eat everything on their plates but had 'ways and means' of secreting unwanted remnants under a pile of plates. Desserts included 'flies' graveyard' – sweet mincemeat on top of the school's 'chisel pastry'. The Christmas Dinner was 'an eagerly anticipated gastronomic event', particularly as the date was always kept a secret.[36]

Victoria College survived the difficulties of the war years and continued to expand and progress. Mrs Faris paid tribute to her pupils who had helped the staff through these troubled times:

> It is only in the shadow of great events that we realise the world for what it is and ourselves for what the world has made us […] I cannot praise too highly the cheerful interest, the alertness and willing cooperation of the girls through what has been a most difficult year.[37]

VICTORIA COLLEGE AFTER THE WAR

Victoria College in its eighty-six years has come through three wars. Founded just after the Crimean War it is not on record that it was affected to any extent by the Boer War, although Victorians of that day still tell how after the Relief of Ladysmith (February 1900) the students of the Queen's College stormed the entrances to Victoria, surrounded Mrs Byers, and demanded a holiday for the girls. In the 1914–18 War the shadow of the heavy casualty lists darkened the school; but in this war for the first time the school has been directly affected and its daily life and routine altered by the imminence of danger and wartime restrictions.
GRACE FARIS[38]

After the war, Victoria College returned to a normality of sorts. Drumglass House was restored to the school and renovations began. The air raid shelters were removed in the Crescent and, most importantly, the evacuees arrived back in Belfast and the school was reunited. Mrs Faris welcomed the return to routine. She believed that the school had become rather parochial without the resident pupils and that the day girls had 'felt a little lonely' when they saw Drumglass House occupied by strangers. Yet, for the majority of the evacuees this was not a homecoming, but a new and alien experience. Indeed, most of the boarders had never before stepped foot in Drumglass or in the Belfast school, which seemed vast after the two classrooms at Portballintrae. But the transition was made easier by the homely atmosphere at Lower Crescent and the fact it was still a family school – Mrs Faris' sister, Miss Acheson, was a teacher at Victoria; her daughter, Katherine, joined the staff soon thereafter.[39]

In December 1945 the school returned to Drumglass Hall for its annual prize distribution. The Countess of Granville was guest of honour on this momentous occasion. In her annual

Officers of the Girls' Training Corps
attend a course at Victoria College,
News Letter, 15 February 1943.

report, Mrs Faris paid tribute to former pupils who had served in Her Majesty's Forces during the Second World War. The roll of honour included the names of one hundred Old Victorians, thirty-three of whom held commissions. In 1950 an illuminated roll of honour was unveiled, listing the names of 108 pupils who had served and two who had died. It was intended to inspire and set an example to present and future pupils of the school. The illuminated lettering was undertaken by the renowned Ulster artist, Mercy Hunter, who was head of the art department from 1947 until 1970.[40] Mrs Faris spoke of the feeling of great relief that the war had ended, and also of the changes war had brought, particularly the vast increase in numbers. Like other schools in the city, Victoria now had its highest number of pupils on record, its largest sixth form ever, and the boarding department was full. The pressing need for more classroom space unfortunately led to the closure of the secretarial department and the relocation of the Froebel Department to 17 Malone Road, where it continued until 1956.

Otherwise, school life returned to normal. Societies were blossoming and sports flourished. The hockey team was particularly successful in the post-war years, winning the Ulster Schools' Hockey Cup for several years in succession. Social events were enjoyed and the sixth-form dance was an important date in the senior girls' diaries. Many of the girls were invited to the Campbell and Royal Belfast Academical Institution (RBAI) dances. In November 1949 it was Victoria's turn to host the sixth-form dance, which was held in Drumglass Hall. Seniors from other Belfast schools were invited and the evening was hailed a great success.[41]

When travel to Europe was once more possible, pupils were encouraged to take part in foreign exchanges to improve their languages. In 1949, seven girls stayed with families in France, and they wrote short reports of their experiences for *The Victorian* magazine.

The school retained close links with its former pupils and in December 1948 the renowned medievalist, Helen Waddell, was invited to distribute the prizes and address the girls. She was presented with a gift by the head girl, Brenda Kenyon, who some thirty years later was appointed headmistress of Victoria College.

MRS FARIS AND HER STAFF

A contemporary has said that the main function of the headmistress is to listen – to listen to the girls, to colleagues, to parents, to governors, to His Majesty's inspectors. But once a year, in presenting her annual report, the headmistress speaks. Having done so, I shall now relapse into my customary silence for the next twelve months.

GRACE FARIS[42]

The memories of former pupils offer a glimpse of daily life during Mrs Faris' headship and evoke the kindness, eccentricities and formidableness of a number of staff who left their imprint on those whom they taught. Mrs Faris was a brilliant scholar and an inspiring teacher, but she was remembered above all for her great humanity and common sense. She knew each pupil by name and gave everyone the same consideration, regardless of whether she (or he) was a senior member of the teaching staff or the 'smallest and grubbiest girl'.[43] While Mrs Faris excelled at mathematics, she had a breadth of learning. Senior classes might expect an impromptu Classics or English lesson from their headmistress if their regular teacher happened to be absent; this was always a rousing experience. Several former pupils recall their monthly meeting in her office to receive their reports. The girls were called form by form and given encouragement and advice. For the younger classes there was an added delight, since the pupil with the best report earned the privilege of blowing the wooden whistle that sounded like a cuckoo.[44] Mrs Faris' love of music led to the formation of the school orchestra in 1936. She would often accompany the girls on her violin when they performed at functions, and she made time to attend the practices despite her many other duties. Astrid Maddock (née McMath) remembers one particular occasion when Mrs Faris and the orchestra accompanied a dance routine in Drumglass Hall. A group of girls dressed in Grecian-style tunics performed a graceful routine that involved throwing balls to each other. By the end of their performance most of the balls had landed in the orchestra, but the sea of dancers' arms continued to wave.[45]

SAINTS AND SINNERS

To many a householder the words 'Miss Smyth says' is the unanswerable and ultimate authority in culinary matters and against which words there is no appeal … What Miss Smyth says goes.

M.G. MCN[46]

The domestic goddess-cum-dragon of Victoria College was undoubtedly Miss Smyth, who ruled supreme over the domestic-science department for thirty-two years, until her retirement

Mrs Faris and senior pupils at Lower Crescent

in 1952. Miss Smyth insisted on high standards and was intolerant of carelessness. At the end of each class she would embark on a rigorous inspection of the room to ensure that all the wooden implements, including the tables, had been thoroughly scrubbed. The girls awaited their turn in trepidation, since failure to meet the required standards resulted in a repeat scrubbing. The girls' written work was scrutinised with equal vigour. Every statement had to be explained and those who neglected to do so would find their margins peppered with the word 'Why?' written in red ink. Miss Smyth issued buttonholes, not lines. Fines were imposed on any girl who forgot her apron or cap or had committed the unspeakable and put her feet on the white-painted rungs of the table. The proceeds went to charity. If any miscreant was unable to pay her fine, she was instead given hemming to do after school, but would be consoled with biscuits and warm milk, for despite her 'seeming severity', Miss Smyth had a genuine interest in the welfare of the girls – and that of their future husbands. Miss Smyth was wont to say that she had saved many a man from an ulcer. She compiled two cookery books, which were a bedrock for many former pupils, guiding them through marriage and motherhood. They contained recipes and household hints and, as Joyce Moran claims, could be described as a 'Bride's Bible'. She still has copies of both books, which have served her well over the years.[47]

Domestic-science class *c*.1930

Miss Smyth's partner in crime in the domestic-science department was Miss Thompson, 'an alert little Scots woman also noted for her fondness for perfection'. Sewing that did not meet Miss Thompson's standards had to be ripped out and redone until it was deemed neat. Perfection was required of any sample to be placed in the girls' specimen books. For their Senior Certificate practical, the girls had to model a dress they had painstakingly made for the inspector.[48] Fortunately, and particularly for Betty Kerr (née Henderson), this was not required of juniors, whose first project was to make a pair of large, pink knickers. Miss Thompson monitored the girls' progress closely and would call up each individually to inspect her work. Betty can still recall her mortification after Miss Thompson examined her handiwork and called the girls to order to 'see what this silly girl has done' – Betty had sewn both legs together.[49]

For Astrid Maddocks, Mrs Ruby Phillips (née Steele) stood out most clearly in her mind. With 'a stentorian bellow and a heart of gold', she was larger than life in every way:

> Her voice would have silenced a parade ground and when she
> laughed, ripples travelled down her many folds of chins – but she
> was great [...] and gave me a real love of the Latin language.[50]

Mrs Phillips' classes made a lasting impression on other pupils, who found her lessons stimulating and enterprising. Isobel Kirkwood (née Kerr) recalls Mrs Phillips' great powers of description that vividly conjured up the 'hustle and bustle' of Ancient Rome to each class of girls. Mrs Phillips also regaled them with stories from her travels in Argentina and Canada. Isobel, 'never having left the shores of Northern Ireland', was particularly astonished to learn that in Argentina it was possible to plan a picnic weeks in advance and be sure that the weather would be fine.[51] Mrs Phillips taught Classics, history and English literature, had a vast breadth of knowledge and held firm opinions that she was not afraid to voice. But it was, above all, for her generosity that she was remembered – 'she was for ever giving and would accept nothing in return'.[52]

Other memorable characters included Miss Beattie, the mathematics teacher, who would charge into the classroom late for her lesson, 'gown billowing out behind her and only dimly seen through a cloud of smoke'. The French mistress, Miss Meredith, was renowned for an explosive personality tempered with great kindness. Miss Meredith was originally from Dublin but joined the staff at Victoria College after the war. Upon arriving in Belfast she felt it her mission 'to propagate civilisation among the savages of the North' and 'inculcate a sound knowledge of French grammar among the middle forms of Victoria College'. Miss Meredith gave the girls real French magazines, which they regarded as trophies, and had a passion for travel, which she shared with her pupils and colleagues, even organising a budget honeymoon for one young member of the teaching staff who had never been abroad. A small village near Innsbruck was selected as an appropriate destination and accommodation was duly booked. The newlyweds were rather surprised to meet a member of the teaching staff shopping in Innsbruck on the first day of their honeymoon and wondered, was this part of Miss Meredith's check-up system?[53]

THE MAN IN VICTORIA – PALMER

No Victorian was more deeply imbued with the spirit of the school.
He had become part of that spirit.[54]
R.M.H.

One figure who stood at the heart of Victoria and was described as the pillar of the school was Mr William Palmer, janitor from 1928 until his death in 1967 and known to all as Palmer. Palmer had worked under three headmistresses and claimed these had been happy times, although he and Miss Matier had occasionally 'fought the piece out'.[55] It was Miss Matier who called him Palmer rather than William or Mr Palmer, and to him she was Madam, 'five foot nothing in size three shoes; slim with rosy cheeks'. For thirty-nine years and, indeed, until the day before his death, Palmer 'guarded the interests of Victoria College as loyally as any Old Victorian'.[56] With his 'cap, worn with the peak to the back, the pipe and the aroma of "Walnut Slice"', Palmer made sure that the school was cleaned and kept in good repair, that the brown lino was well polished, and that doors and windows could shut without banging.[57] He opened the school for special functions and lit a roaring fire for the OGA reunions in the lecture hall. Palmer witnessed many events and changes in Victoria College. He remembered the school

Palmer at the door of the Lower
Crescent school

without electricity or central heating. Then, classrooms were lit by single gas jets and 'it was the
school versus the gym-mistress' when it came to heating, for each morning the gym mistress
would stand with her back to the newly stoked boiler and remain there until Palmer returned
to re-stoke it. He recalled the fire in the gym in 1937, the flood in the lecture hall on the very
morning of a public examination and the week of the centenary celebrations in 1959, when
he was presented with a wallet and cheque from the OGA in recognition of his loyal service
to the school.

Old girls returning to Victoria would invariably ask if Palmer was still around – he
was an institution. A former pupil and member of the teaching staff explained that when she
herself had been a girl, Palmer was less talkative with the children than later, when he was an
adoring and indulgent grandfather rather than a strict father of two girls. Hence, 'the present

generation have come closer to twisting him around their little fingers than we ever did'. Palmer was and still is remembered with great love and affection by generations of Victorians. He occasionally grumbled, but as one pupil remarked, what man would not who had to work among six hundred females on a daily basis. Palmer had hoped to see the school through its relocation to the new site, but he died in 1967, having worked until the last and shown tremendous loyalty and devotion for almost forty years. As Miss Cunningham explained:

> He had grown old with the building and seemed to have a kinship
> with it […] he guarded the interests of Victoria College as loyally as
> any Old Victorian.[58]

THE 1947 EDUCATION ACT: THE BEGINNING OF A NEW REGIME

To hold what is best is the legacy of the past and to jettison lumber
was a good beginning for any reform.
GRACE FARIS[59]

In her annual report for 1944 Mrs Faris alluded to the imminent changes in education which she hoped would produce an educated nation, and not simply a literate one. While Mrs Faris acknowledged that change, 'even from worse to better', did not happen without inconvenience, she was concerned that the great traditions of Ulster's secondary schools should not be lost in the process.[60] War delayed reform, but in 1947 a new education act was implemented, modelled on the 1944 Education Act in England and Wales. This sought to create the first nationwide system of state-funded education and introduced the qualifying examination for eleven-year-olds; those who passed were entitled to continue their education at a grammar school, regardless of their parents' financial situation. Speaking at the annual prize distribution in 1948, the Reverend Dr John Waddell, chairman of the Victoria College board of governors, welcomed the opportunities afforded by the Education Act, since this offered all intelligent children, whatever their background, the chance to get 'an outlook into the bigger world which science, history, literature and imagination reveal'. Others had reservations and Mrs Faris was concerned that the traditions of the grammar schools might be lost in 'a mass-produced education'. Still, she was confident that this would be avoided at Victoria College given the individuality of the girls and the teachers' determination to prevent 'a conveyor belt' system.[61]

The immediate and most striking impact of the new act was increased numbers and pressure for places. There was now a greater demand for a grammar school education, and while Victoria responded to the Ministry of Education's mandate to increase its intake – and the school was noticeably fuller – many applicants had to be turned away. Whereas previously there had been three applicants for each place, there were now six.

There were further changes. In return for public funding to subsidise pupils' fees and help with building work, the board of governors was required to abdicate many of its rights to the state. Thus the staff-to-pupil ratio would now be decided by the Ministry of Education, who would also stipulate how many non-qualified pupils could be admitted. The level of state intervention proposed was on a totally new scale and it alarmed a number of schools, including Victoria College, Campbell College and RBAI. They feared for their traditions and were concerned that the reforms would destroy the sense of pride and responsibility they felt in running their own schools. But the consequences for opting out were serious – schools that rejected the scheme would forfeit scholarships for their qualified pupils. After many serious discussions and much hard thought, Victoria College and twelve other schools rejected the proposals. The board of governors explained that it was compelled to make this decision as it feared for Victoria's freedom and independence.

The schools that opted out of the Ministry's scheme formed a deputation under Austin Brown, chair of the board of RBAI. Following a number of lengthy discussions the group presented its concerns to the Ministry of Education and explained that while each of them wished to play a part in the 1947 reforms, they were concerned to protect and preserve the history and traditions of their respective schools. After 'frank and friendly discussion', a compromise was reached. Those who opted out would be known as voluntary B grammar schools. They would sacrifice their 65 per cent capital-expenditure grant to subsidise building work, but would now receive state scholarships for all qualified pupils and, crucially, would retain 'a measure of freedom in educational policy and financial control' which they had previously enjoyed. The board of governors of Victoria College paid tribute to the tremendous efforts of Austin Brown and, also, to the support of the parents of the school, who during the uncertainty had agreed to stand by the board's decision and meet the costs of their daughters' fees if necessary.[62] For Mrs Faris, this had been the most difficult year for the school since Dr Byers' death in 1912, when the future of Victoria College had hung in the balance. But the school had risen to the challenge and weathered another storm. As Mary Moore, the registrar of Victoria College, commented in 1952:

> A great school is not made up of bricks and mortar. No Chancellor of
> the Exchequer nor financial crisis will ever be able to curtail our building
> programme. The fabric of our world is maintained by those countless girls
> and women who may not have attained greatness but who have at some
> time or another during their short school life here caught a glimpse
> of something greater than themselves.[63]

'WE ARE BUT A GENERATION; THE SCHOOL GOES ON'[64]

Wit without malice, culture and scholarship worn lightly, organising
ability of the highest order, true kindliness […] Perhaps most important
of all, she had an obvious love for the school and all its pupils.
E.A.G.[65]

In 1951 Mrs Faris retired as headmistress of the school, but retained an active and lively interest in it. She continued as president of the OGA until her death in December 1973. From 1956 until 1968 Mrs Faris was a member of the board of governors, and was succeeded by her son, Professor John Faris. Mrs Faris brought the school through a war, she met the challenges

OPENING OF NEW SUN NURSERY AT VICTORIA HOMES, BALLYSILLAN, BELFAST. — Photograph taken in the sun nursery after the opening ceremony by Mrs. G. Faris, M.A. (on right), principal of Victoria College, on Saturday. Also included are Lady Turner, Mrs. Russell (who presided), Mrs. G. Wilson, and Miss Morris (lady superintendent of the Homes).

The opening of the Sun Nursery at the Victoria Homes, 31 October 1938. Mrs Faris is on the far right.

of extensive educational reforms but, above all, maintained the traditions of Victoria College while responding to change. She was remembered by her former pupils and colleagues with great affection. They paid tribute to her initiative, scholarship and generous spirit. The fact that sixteen of Mrs Faris' staff remained at the school throughout her headship is a testimony to the respect and devotion she inspired.

In January 1952 the OGA presented T.C. Dugdale's portrait of Mrs Faris to the school. Those who attended the unveiling reflected on how future generations who had never known the principal would assess her from the painting:

> And what of the portrait itself? It portrays a grave and thoughtful
> scholar, perhaps sterner than the Mrs Faris with whom we are familiar,
> but as we look closer we notice the beginning of a smile and then we
> recognise the Mrs Faris we love. [66]

Coat of arms

The coat of arms

*Per Pale Sanguine and Sable on the dexter a harp
Or on the sinster an open book proper edged and
bound gold a chief vair thereon a pale
Azure charged with a Bee Argent*

BLAZON, VICTORIA COLLEGE COAT OF ARMS, 1951

In 1951 the College of Arms in London granted
Victoria College a coat of arms (an armorial
achievement). This was to replace the old school
badge but would incorporate the school's motto
'*Honor, fidelitatis praemium*' ('Honour is the reward of
faithfulness'), which was formally adopted in 1923.[67]

The old school badge

The galleon of Richmond Lodge School

The evolution of design

The emblems or devices that appear on the shield (escutcheon) of the 1951 coat of arms are a gold harp shown on a red (sanguine) background, an open book on a black (sable) background and a silver bee against a blue (azure) background. On either side of the bee there is what looks to be a series of bells, but which in fact represents the pattern formed by the vairs, namely the pieces of blue–grey and white squirrel skin which were sewn alternately in cup-shaped patches. The choice of emblems is significant. The open book, which may in fact be the Bible, represents learning and is fitting for an educational institution. The other elements are drawn from the old school badge, which comprised a harp (the heraldic emblem of Belfast), a crown and the initials MB for Margaret Byers. The harp reappears in the coat of arms and is an obvious import from the badge. More subtle is the inclusion of the bee, for while it symbolises industry and the work ethos of Victoria College, it also stands for the first letter of the founder's name, Byers, and is thus a pictorial representation of the MB on the badge.

Following the amalgamation of Victoria College and Richmond Lodge School in 1987, it was decided to modify the coat of arms to represent this merger. Patricia Pyne, senior teacher and a member of the board of governors, was made responsible for redesigning the coat of arms and acquiring permission for its alteration from the Norroy and Ulster King of Arms. The design incorporates a galleon, the emblem of Richmond Lodge School, which is mentioned in the Richmond School song. But, as Patricia Pyne has suggested, the galleon may symbolise a young person setting out on the voyage of life; an appropriate motif for a school. At this time it was also decided that the new coat of arms should adopt a more elaborate form. Thus, a helmet is shown on the top of the shield and ornate mantling or drapery (lambrequin), which represents the protective cloth or scarf worn by the knight to deflect enemy wounds and shield him from the elements.[68]

The school flag

In 2000 Victoria College acquired its own flag, which displays the school's coat of arms and motto. This was the initiative of Professor David Hadden, chairman of the board of governors, who presented the flag to the school to mark the end of his office. In 2008 it was decided to commission a special sesquicentennial flag to commemorate the 150th anniversary of Victoria College, to be flown during the celebratory year. This was organised by the assistant principal Hilary Woods and the Anniversary Celebration Committee. On 8 January 2009 the anniversary celebrations were launched with the raising of this flag by Lady Carswell OBE, lord lieutenant of Belfast and a former head girl of Victoria (1951–2). The ceremony was attended by pupils, parents, staff, governors and members of the OGA. The flag displays the dates 1859–2009 beneath the school coat of arms and motto. Both flags were made by the Bannerman Flag Company, Belfast.

The raising of the sesquicentennial flag by Lady Carswell OBE, 8 January 2009. Also in the photograph are Mr Christopher Maccabe, chair of the board of governors, and Ms Patricia Slevin, headmistress.

Miss Cunningham and the relocation to Cranmore Park, 1951–76

Miss Cunningham and a
young pupil, 1959

We have revelled in our past glories but we have not lost sight of the need to plan.

WEIR CUNNINGHAM[1]

Miss Weir Cunningham was the first headmistress of Victoria College who had not been a pupil or a member of the teaching staff. Yet she was moved by the same spirit as her predecessors, and believed in promoting a liberal education for girls and advancing the school in accordance with current demands. While deeply proud of Victoria's traditions, Miss Cunningham was forward-thinking and progressive. But her headship was difficult from the outset; as one former pupil reflected, it was 'a little like an obstacle race'.[2] There were major changes in the examination system, negotiations regarding the school's status, and problems with space that led to a building project in the Crescent and eventually to the relocation of the school. Not least there were anxieties and inconveniences caused by the Troubles. Nevertheless, there was opportunity for jubilation with the celebration of the school's centenary in 1959 and the Golden October week of festivities.

WEIR CUNNINGHAM: 'THE UNREPENTANT ACADEMIC'[3]

Forward-looking, fresh in mind, calm and appreciative, this headmistress considers the stresses and problems of present-day education for girls with the good-tempered certainty that a rational and imaginative approach must lead to solutions of good sense.

NEWS LETTER[4]

When Miss Cunningham succeeded Mrs Faris in 1951 she was not yet thirty-eight years of age. She was a graduate of Trinity College Dublin, having obtained a First Class Honours degree in French and German. Prior to her appointment as headmistress, Miss Cunningham was senior modern languages mistress at King's Norton Grammar School, Birmingham, but she had previously taught at Methodist College, Belfast, and undertaken welfare work in post-war Europe. Although Miss Cunningham herself had no previous ties with Victoria College, a relative, Miss Margaret Cunningham, had taught at the school in the early nineteenth century and officiated briefly as Mrs Byers' vice principal.

It was a difficult task for anyone to fill Mrs Faris' shoes, but Miss Cunningham soon won the respect and affection of her pupils and colleagues, who paid tribute to her integrity, her sense of humour and the liberal environment she maintained. She was fair, diplomatic and, importantly, had the great ability of distinguishing the significant from the trivial and permitting changes that would satisfy current trends without undermining the ethos of the school. Thus, the prefect system that in 1971 was considered outdated was replaced by the Sixth-form Council. This meant that all the upper-sixth girls shared responsibility for running the school and wore the special tie hitherto reserved for prefects. Prior to this the prefects'

Miss Cunningham enjoys a dance with
a preparatory pupil, 1959

Mrs Mortimer, Miss Glen and the
Drumglass Kindergarten, 1959

dance had been changed to the sixth-form formal and final-year pupils were allowed to wear their own clothes in their last term as preparation for university.[5] Indeed, Miss Cunningham firmly believed in moving with the times and was amazed at one headmaster's surprise that the female teachers of Victoria College wore trousers.[6] Salie Tinsley (née Thompson), who was head girl in 1958–9, recalls her own experience of Miss Cunningham's wittiness. This was in December 1957, following a rehearsal for *The Taming of the Shrew*. Salie had been cast as the shrew, a part she played 'with fiery venom', but she lost her voice immediately before the practice performance and was deeply upset on the car journey home. She was, however, slightly taken aback and even shocked when her driver, Miss Cunningham, expressed her sympathy, adding 'and the part suits you so well'.[7]

Like Dr Byers, Miss Cunningham had a great love of children and treasured her weekly visits to the preparatory department. She was an enthusiastic participant at their parties and joined in the games and dancing with great gusto. The young pupils equally cherished these visits and the personal attention they received from their headmistress. Susan Faulkner (née Mashal) recalls that any pupil who was celebrating her birthday on the day of Miss Cunningham's weekly visit would be invited to sit on the headmistress' knee at assembly. One little girl who was keen to demonstrate her prowess in skipping was patiently watched by Miss Cunningham until she reached her one hundredth jump. At this point the headmistress heartily congratulated her, but suggested she might take a well-deserved rest.[8]

Miss Cunningham was a much-respected figure outside the school and played an active role in educational developments in Northern Ireland. Notably, she was a governor of Stranmillis College, Belfast, and the Northern Ireland Polytechnic, and was on the Education Advisory Committee of UTV.

DAILY LIFE IN THE LOWER CRESCENT

Tolerance and a sense of humour oiled the wheels of her administration
[…] to the youngest she was no awe-inspiring figure, nor to the older girls
a martinet.
NORAH WATTS, 1977[9]

When Miss Cunningham first visited the Lower Crescent school as an interviewee for the headship, she was immediately drawn to the old building with its maze of corridors and stairways, its crumbling walls and cracks in the ceilings. The building was steeped in character and fostered the 'closely-knit happy community' that a school inspector described following his visit to Victoria College in 1955.[10] The school was homely, particularly in winter when a large fire was lit in the lecture hall for evening functions. To the new girl, this labyrinth could be rather bewildering and take some time to master, but soon thereafter the advantages were realised. The lower third cloakroom in the bowels of the school was 'a cavern furnished with rows of hooks and brightly painted metal boxes for shoes' and offered great opportunities for off-ground tig. The large clock in the reception hall, which had once belonged to Dr Byers, was a useful place to secrete a petticoat and other illicit items.[11]

The school day began with a short assembly at 9 a.m. Free milk was distributed at the

11 a.m. break and classes finished after 3 p.m. Occasionally the school welcomed a guest speaker. One who made a deep impression on Jennifer Breene (née Lapham) was the missionary Gladys Aylward, who visited in September 1963. Jennifer was struck by how small Gladys was as she progressed past the line of girls at morning assembly and remembers vividly how she spoke of her work with children in China. The talk had a lasting effect and later, when Jennifer was a teacher at the school, she would read extracts of Gladys' biography, *The Small Woman*, to P7 pupils.

Others recall the impact of national and international affairs on school life. One such momentous occasion was the death of George VI in 1952. Jeannie Hall remembers when the news was broken at the school assembly; it was greeted with 'a stunned silence' and some of the younger girls were reduced to tears.[12] The coronation of Elizabeth II in June 1953 was marked by a three-day holiday and by the planting of flowers and trees in both the Crescent playground and at Drumglass House. The head girl and her deputy joined a party of schoolgirls to attend the celebrations in London.[13] Radios were strictly forbidden in the hall, but an exception was made at critical times, such as during the Cuban Missile Crisis in the early 1960s 'when the fate of the world stood in the balance'.[14]

Numbers at the school continued to grow and in 1959, Victoria's centenary year, there were five hundred and fifty girls, fifty-seven of whom were boarders. During the sixties, numbers rose significantly in the sixth form. This was a direct consequence of the introduction of GCE examinations, since more girls now stayed on after Ordinary level (O level). In 1974, when the school reopened at Cranmore Park, there were six hundred and seventy pupils on the register.

Entrance to Victoria College was based upon the applicant's qualifying result, and also on her performance in a school test. Every effort was made to ensure that girls were selected on merit alone, although preference was given to those who had sisters at the school so that families would not be separated. Miss Cunningham interviewed every single applicant, whether she was a four-year-old hoping to join the preparatory department or an eleven-year-old candidate for the senior school, for she believed in knowing and being known by all of her pupils.[15] While Miss Cunningham commanded respect throughout the school, she was approachable and quick to show compassion. Dorothy Walsh (née Chambers) joined the boarding department when she was ten years old and was at first terribly homesick. One day she ventured to the school office, hoping that she might be allowed to telephone home. Dorothy was duly shown into the headmistress' study, where she was invited to sit on Miss Cunningham's knee while she rang her mother. Years later, when Dorothy joined the Old Girls' Association (OGA), Miss Cunningham reminded her of this incident.[16]

SOCIETIES AND SPORTS

School societies were formed, disbanded and reformed according to current trends and interests. In 1954 the first members of the Scientific Society enjoyed a ramble on Cave Hill, fishing in rock pools and a tour of Richardson's Chemical Manure Works. When Spanish was introduced to the curriculum by Mrs Millicent Cromie, a Spanish Circle was duly formed. Various societies organised joint meetings with other schools and in 1968 the choirs of Victoria

The First Eleven, winners of the Ulster
Schools' Cup, 1972 with Mrs Templeton,
Miss Cunningham and Mrs Morrison

College and the Royal Belfast Academical Institution came together for the first time to give a performance of the Fauré *Requiem*. This was the first of many collaborative productions and, as Miss Cunningham explained, the practices were as enjoyable as the performance.[17] Social services and charity work continued to be an important part of school life and links with the Victoria Homes were retained until *c.*1980, when the organisation was restructured.

Sport had always been central to the school curriculum and remained so during Miss Cunningham's headship. New clubs were formed for girls wishing to take part in badminton, table tennis and gymnastics after school, while netball was introduced as a second winter sport. Cricket was played each week from May until September, and although there was not a school team as such (this was formed in 1988), a number of Victoria girls were prominent members of the Belfast Women's Cricket Club, and often took on the men's teams. As one pupil remarked, 'a bevy of glamorous belles show the amazed mere males that cricket can be played by the fairer sex who can on occasion manage to win by guile, if not skill'.[18] Annual fixtures included sports days, galas and inter-school competitions. There was often staff participation at these events and in 1971 a relay team comprising Mrs Cromie, Mrs Wilson, Miss Kane, Mrs Jordan, Dr Acheson and Mr Goldsmith donned nightgowns over their swimsuits and stormed to victory in a freestyle race against the head girl, her deputy and the four House captains.[19]

While a number of sports were played, hockey and tennis remained most popular. There were some great successes. At the start of Miss Cunningham's headship the tennis team won the 1953 Ulster Senior Schools' Cup and retained this for the following two years. In the early seventies, the First Eleven dominated Ulster schools' hockey, and there was great jubilation in 1972 when the team, captained by Marilyn Dawson, defeated Strathearn 3–2 to win the Ulster Senior Hockey Cup for the first time in twenty-one years. A thousand pupils watched this exciting match and the entire school was given a half-day holiday to celebrate the team's victory. Miss Cunningham, who was herself a keen hockey supporter, treated the First Eleven and the PE staff to a celebratory dinner, along with Mr Tommy McDowell, the groundsman. Mr McDowell had always taken a great interest in the school's hockey and had even travelled with the team to matches. The girls felt it was fitting that in his final year as groundsman they should bring back the cup. The following year the First Eleven shared the cup with Ballymena Academy and enjoyed a celebratory meal in Portballintrae, courtesy of Dr Maclaine, who owned a hotel there and whose daughter, Sallie, was captain of the team. 1974 was another remarkable year for hockey with Victoria College providing captains for the Ulster School and Senior teams, the Irish Intermediate team and the English and Irish University teams. The *News Letter* declared this 'an outstanding record for any school'.[20]

An important figure at this time was Mrs Winifred Templeton, or Mrs T as she was affectionately known. A former pupil of the school, Mrs Templeton was a founder member of the Victorians' Hockey Club, honorary secretary of the OGA for over thirty years and, not least, an internationally renowned umpire. She officiated as both coach and umpire in school hockey and tennis, and took a keen interest in the girls' progress, but insisted upon neatness and good manners at all times. Following her death in December 1976 the Victorians' Hockey Club and the OGA started a fund in Mrs Templeton's name to raise money for a hockey pavilion. They received help from both the board of governors and the Ministry of Education and on 24 April 1985 the Templeton Pavilion was opened by Michael Scott, Minister for Education in Northern Ireland.[21]

THE SCHOOL TRIP

Never has so much been done for so many by so few
WINSTON CHURCHILL[22]

Victoria College has always encouraged pupils to travel to improve their languages and broaden their cultural experiences. From Dr Byers' days the school arranged for girls to attend foreign language courses, to work as au pairs and to participate in exchanges. In June 1938 two parties of pupils were brought to the Glasgow Exhibition, one group of seventy girls and another of twenty. This was seemingly the first organised group visit, but it was really in the 1960s that the school trip became a fixture in the Victoria College calendar. A number of these trips was led by Miss Mary Boucher and her first was to Amsterdam in 1961. All her trips were organised with precision, and she would even check beforehand if any girl had a birthday while they were away and ensure there was a little present and card for her on the morning of her celebration. Pupils soon had an opportunity to travel the world. There were literary pilgrimages around England, trips to European capitals and cruises around the Mediterranean. Mrs Patricia Pyne recalls a particularly memorable cruise in 1981 when she and Mrs Rosemary Wilson accompanied a school party on the SS *Uganda*. While the group followed the wonderful itinerary, there was hysteria in Belfast, for a hoax caller to a local radio station reported that the cruise ship had gone down in the Mediterranean. The girls' parents were frantic, but the group was 'blissfully unaware of the drama playing itself out at home'.[23]

The school party on board the
SS *Uganda*, 1981

For many pupils, the school trip was their first opportunity to leave Northern Ireland and experience travel by boat or plane. It was also a chance for the girls to see the sights of London and most trips therefore broke their journey in the capital. While travel is now much more widespread and many pupils enjoy foreign and exotic holidays with their families and friends, the school trip remains an important and integral part of the school experience, both for pupils and staff. A variety of opportunities and experiences is offered. There are geography field-trips, art-history trips, ski trips and joint ventures with other schools. In 1989 a group of sixth-form pupils from ten schools in Northern Ireland embarked on an educational trip to Berlin, where they interviewed residents on both sides of the Wall literally days before it came down. In the early 1990s several parties of girls from Victoria College and St Dominic's enjoyed French cuisine trips to Hardelot in northern France, where they watched cookery demonstrations and sampled fine fare.[24]

School trips are not always memorable for the right reasons. Mrs Judy Young, former head of modern languages and inveterate school-tripper, recalls how problems with pupils' visas and health led to overnight stays in airports and hospitals, while staff quarters were rarely luxurious. In one small hotel in France, Judy and her colleagues had to share beds since all the twin-bedded rooms had been allocated to the Argentinean Under-nineteen Rugby Team.[25]

THE TEACHING STAFF

*One of the most satisfying experiences is to see the light of understanding in
a child's eye. It's like an actor getting across to an audience from the stage.*
WEIR CUNNINGHAM[26]

Miss Cunningham remarked on the continuity of teaching staff at Victoria College. Most
teachers remained at the school for their entire career; those who left did so as a consequence
of marriage, maternity or maturity. This created stability and fostered a sense of community.
Miss Lindsay, 'a small indomitable figure' who taught English from 1945 until 1974, made a
great impression on her pupils. She 'stood for no nonsense', insisted on high standards and was
both feared and respected. From years of experience, Miss Lindsay had a shrewd understanding
of pupils' ploys. Ann Kirkpatrick (née Blair) recalls how she and her classmates were amazed
when Miss Lindsay cannily exposed a fellow pupil who was 'reciting' her poetry homework
from words stuck on the back of another girl. At their next lesson, mathematics with Mrs Ardill,
they discovered that one of Mrs Ardill's classmates had attempted a similar ruse many years
before; on that occasion a misreading of 'onion' for 'union' had revealed the trickery.[27] Miss
Eileen McAlister, 'a Victorian of the Victorians', was head of history and, later, vice principal.

Mercy Hunter and her art class, 1959

She was erudite, extremely kind and also, as Barbara Farris (née Cumins) discovered, had an unexpected passion for driving – and at speed. When Barbara had a subject clash during her A-level examinations, Miss McAlister was made responsible for supervising her over the lunch period, to ensure that she did not meet any of the other candidates. Barbara had hardly anticipated that at lunchtime she would be driven by Miss McAlister 'at a surprising speed' to her home, where the housekeeper had prepared a sumptuous spread.[28] Dr Rose McLernon, head of modern languages and vice principal, retired in 1965 after thirty-five years on the teaching staff. She was acknowledged as one of the best language teachers in Ulster and introduced the girls 'to a new language and a new world'. She also taught English to the allied troops during the war. Dr McLernon showed great generosity and compassion and on several occasions offered to lend pupils money to finance their university education, with the understanding that they might or might not pay this back; a remarkable act of kindness.[29]

One figure who stood larger than life in the school – and arguably in Northern Ireland – was Mercy Hunter MBE, who was head of the art department from 1947 until 1970. Mercy was an established artist and a co-founder of the Ulster Society of Women Artists, and she was also well known in Northern Ireland literary circles. She was particularly close to Louis MacNeice, and it was his wife who gave Tara the Afghan hound to Mercy. Tara was a frequent visitor to Lower Crescent and the subject of many of the girls' artistic creations. Mercy's studio in the school was on the upper floor and had a wonderful panoramic view of the city. This was painted many times by her classes, along with countless potted plants. She was 'no ordinary teacher' and her studio was equally unique. There were two cupboards named Chinatown and Bluebeard; while the raw materials for artistic endeavours were kept in the former, the latter was 'a sanctum only to be entered by express permission'.[30]

Mercy is remembered as an inspiring teacher who, it was said, could get art out of a stone. She was concerned to expand her pupils' artistic knowledge and skills and thus taught them art history and calligraphy. She also took them to many galleries and exhibitions.[31] A colourful figure in the staffroom, Mercy was renowned for her lavish hospitality. One former colleague would often recount the fate of a fellow diner who, unused to Mercy's generous measures, slipped further down her chair with each glass of wine poured; by the end of the evening, she was literally under the table.[32] A striking, and perhaps surprising image of Mercy is of her standing in goal, keenly defending the interests of East House at the inter-House hockey matches. Following Mercy's death in 1989, the OGA and school planted a weeping willow tree outside Drumglass House in her memory.[33]

1959: 'THE GOLDEN OCTOBER WEEK OF THE CENTENARY'[34]

We were carried along by a sort of spiritual levitation and unweariedly
from one scene of celebration to another.

E. MAUD FARRINGTON (NÉE WHITE)[35]

The approach of the school's centenary was anticipated with much excitement and forward planning. In 1957 a centenary committee was established to organise celebratory events and to compile a history of the school.[36] Several members of the committee interviewed former pupils, some of whom had been taught by Dr Byers and were among the earliest graduates of the collegiate department. The OGA set up a Centenary Fund to provide an all-weather hockey pitch for the school, since the grass pitch suffered endless problems with flooding. The OGA acknowledged Dr Byers' other 'foundation' on this occasion and presented the Victoria Homes with a picture and a piano. In 1986, following the closure of the Homes, the picture was returned to the school along with a portrait of Margaret Byers.[37]

The centenary was marked with a week of celebrations that began on Sunday 11 October with a service of thanksgiving in Fisherwick Church attended by a congregation of 1,400. The festivities concluded on Saturday 17 October with a school dance in Drumglass Hall. Throughout the week there were performances of a school pageant that was specially written by Dr Byers' great niece, Jean Baxter, who starred as the founder. The preparatory department had its own party complete with a cake and games, and the OGA marked the occasion with a special centenary reunion dinner held at the Woodbourne House Hotel and a dinner dance in the Floral Hall. An open day provided an opportunity for pupils, parents and friends to tour the school buildings and enjoy the various displays, exhibitions and musical entertainments. Also during the week, a commemorative plaque was unveiled by the former pupil and renowned sculptress, Anne Acheson CBE, and an evening function in Drumglass Hall was attended by Lady Wakehurst, whose husband was at this time Governor of Northern Ireland.

On Friday 16 October there was a special centenary prize distribution in the Whitla Hall at Queen's. Almost a thousand attended this impressive ceremony, where the guest of honour was Lady Keir, a former member of the board of governors. Special awards were presented to three ladies who had been pupils at the school during Dr Byers' headship and who had distinguished themselves as pioneers in their own right. They were Melissa Hull, who was the first female professor in Brazil; Annie McMordie, a long-serving and much-beloved teacher at Victoria College; and Eva Maguire, who had devoted her life to the service of the Sandes Soldiers' and Airmen's Homes and had met Florence Nightingale shortly before her death in 1910.

On the Saturday of the centenary week, the new hockey pitch was officially opened by Mrs Faris, president of the OGA and patron of the Victorians' Hockey Club. Unfortunately, the heavens also opened that day and there was a deluge of rain. While all sporting fixtures in the city were rained off, the match between the Victoria College First Eleven and the Victorians' Hockey Club went ahead, although the latter had to abandon their plan to appear in the long skirts that would have been worn by the school's first hockey team. The match was a resounding victory for the Victorians who won 6–1, but they had a great advantage with two renowned internationalists, Thelma and Moira Hopkins, on their side.

> I do not believe that Victoria College will ever be content to live on her traditions;
> I am confident that its traditions will live and grow in the hands of the generations
> of this its second centenary.
>
> GRACE FARIS [38]

Centenary celebrations, 1959

i   The academic procession arrives at Fisherwick Church

ii   The preparatory department party

iii Members of the cast of the centenary pageant

iv The opening of the all-weather hockey pitch

EDUCATIONAL REFORMS

Culture is dying out and expediency is taking its place. We aim to set forth from our schools not efficient robots, nor yet idealists with their heads in the clouds, but citizens of good sense, integrity and sound principles whose feet are planted firmly on the ground and who should be able to assist in solving the problems of a confused world.

WEIR CUNNINGHAM[39]

The twenty-five years of Miss Cunningham's headship saw considerable changes in education. The new GCE Advanced level (A level) was introduced in the first year she was principal, and the first candidates sat the examinations in June 1952. The A-level course was initially run alongside the Junior and Senior Certificates and offered pupils the opportunity to remain for an extra year at school before going to university. However, the new system made timetabling more complex and exposed the inadequacy of the Ministry's staffing quotas, which Miss Cunningham dismissed as 'completely out of date' and insufficient for any school to cope with the new demands. To make up this shortfall, schools paid for extra teachers from their own limited resources.[40] In spite of the changes, the standard of academic achievement remained high and was particularly noteworthy in 1963, when there was a 100 per cent pass rate at A level and a number of the girls secured the top places in Northern Ireland.[41]

A decade after A levels, the introduction of GCE O level brought more significant changes. This was to replace the Senior Certificate and meant that pupils could now stay at school for seven, rather than six years. But there were serious concerns about this system, which had proved to be flawed in England. Miss Cunningham insisted that Northern Ireland should design its own method of examination and not follow 'slavishly in the wake of England'. She believed that if education was to progress, the state needed to fund working parties of teachers to travel around the world and bring back fresh ideas. But Miss Cunningham's main concern was that the new system was geared for the 'intellectually gifted' and that early specialism would destroy a balanced education. She feared schools would turn out pupils 'with one-track minds, glorified machines' and argued that the entire system ought to be revised to accommodate the non-specialist – a more general course should be offered to those who wished to further their education after O level, but found A level too difficult.[42]

The first O-level examinations were held in 1963, although the new system was introduced gradually over five years. During this period pupils could either take their examinations after six years or after five, as would soon become mandatory. Those who attained the required number of passes could progress to A level. Initially the Junior Certificate examination was continued and taken at the end of three years. This was felt to be 'an unnecessary hurdle in the five-year course to Ordinary' and was stopped in 1964.[43] To counteract the 'evils of specialism', Miss Cunningham introduced a general studies course for sixth formers, to broaden their learning experience and equip them for their dual role as career women and homemakers. The course was not examined and covered a wide range of topics such as judo, cookery and current affairs. During Mrs Berner's headship from 1976 to 1993, the general studies programme was replaced by integrated studies, which was also unexamined. This sought to promote an understanding of world affairs and to keep pupils abreast of current matters.[44]

EXPANSION AND RELOCATION

Victoria, while proud of its traditions, is not content to rest on that alone,
but is moving forward in accordance with the spirit and needs of the age.
KATHERINE FARIS[45]

The old school in Lower Crescent was much loved and, despite its shabbiness, was a source
of great pride in all that it represented. But its 'deficiencies' were becoming increasingly
problematic and Miss Cunningham lived in fear that one of the girls would fall through the
floorboards.[46] Moreover, there was the ongoing problem of a lack of space. Miss Cunningham
and the board of governors continually sought ways to update resources and equip the school
to meet the needs of an ever-changing curriculum. New demands in science teaching and a

Barbara McGibben, Margaret Chalkley
and Norma Cochrane who took the three
top places in A-level biology, 1962

nationwide appeal for scientists prompted the decision in 1955 to build a new science block in the grounds of the Crescent. After much negotiation with the Ministry of Education, the wheels were set in motion and the builders started work. On 23 September 1960 the new science building was opened by Professor Emeleus of Queen's University Belfast, who declared this 'another stage in the growth of the school', and blessed by the Rt Reverend D. Austin Fulton, Moderator of the Presbyterian General Assembly and father of three Victoria pupils. The shiny, hi-tech building housed physics, biology and chemistry laboratories, as well as a sewing room and domestic-science kitchens. The catering for the occasion was produced from these new kitchens.

There were some teething problems with the new science block and initially the odour of strange concoctions from the chemistry laboratory wafted into the domestic-science rooms. The matter was soon resolved with the arrival of 'several large protuberances'.[47] Significantly, just two years after the opening, pupils from Victoria College took the top three places in A-level biology in Northern Ireland. The new resources were clearly a success.

THE MOVE TO CRANMORE PARK

We must not let the past hold back the present and the future, and it is for
the sake of the present Victorians and for those who shall come after them that
we have made this decision … we face the future in the hope and confidence
that the new Victoria College will be worthy of the old.
NORAH WATTS[48]

Despite the extra space afforded by the new science block, it became clear that the school had effectively outgrown the Crescent buildings and would have to relocate. In 1963 Victoria College entered into negotiations with the Ministry of Education and it was decided that a new school to accommodate six or seven hundred pupils should be built in the grounds of Drumglass House. This was not an easy decision to make for the old Crescent building had come to represent Victoria College and it embodied the very essence of the school. The estimated cost of this relocation was £400,000. To meet the expense, the board of governors needed the 65 per cent grant that the Ministry gave voluntary A grammar schools to help with building and equipment. It had little choice but to change Victoria's status from a voluntary B grammar school and to renounce rights it had long struggled to retain. This meant that the state would now have a greater say in the running of the school and could, for example, nominate a third of the members of the board. Mr John Wilson was one of the new board members recommended by the Ministry of Education at this time. He has remained on the board ever since and is one of the longest-serving members in the school's history.

'THE OLD ORDER CHANGETH'[49]

The building stamped its personality on us – the character of a lived-in face
which had survived too many maroon-clad generations to ever be demolished,
at least in the minds of its old inhabitants.

SUSAN MURRAY[50]

The sale of the school at Lower Crescent should have been relatively straightforward, and
also lucrative, given its prime location. However, the move was thrown into disarray in August
1968 when proposals for a ring road were unveiled and showed Victoria College to be in an
affected area. Prospective buyers were driven away and plans for the new school were halted
while the Northern Ireland government deliberated over its legislation on the compensation
for those affected by redevelopment. This was an anxious time for Victoria, but at the end
of November 1969, seven years after the original decision to move had been made, work
began on the new building. In January 1970 the first sod was cut and 'monster machines'
moved into the grounds of Drumglass House, creating a sea of mud. The tranquillity that
the boarding department and the headmistress had hitherto enjoyed ended abruptly. Indeed,
with the school literally on her doorstep, it became essential for the principal to separate
home life from school. Miss Cunningham warned that while anyone visiting her office would
be greeted warmly, those knocking on her front door would likely receive a cool reception.[51]

The architects Shanks and Leighton designed the new school and proposed that it
should be built around Drumglass House and connected via the canteen. Drumglass Hall
would be partitioned, with one section serving as a hall for the preparatory department and
the other as a recreation hall for the boarders. The preparatory department itself was to
consist of six classrooms built in a honeycomb formation. The senior school would be well
equipped and, in addition to classrooms, would have a large assembly hall, a gymnasium,
science laboratories, domestic-science rooms and a language laboratory. Thanks to Miss
Cunningham's hard negotiations with the Ministry of Education, it was also agreed that there
should be a sixth-form centre. She felt this was an important addition which would encourage
a sense of community among the senior girls, foster independence and prepare them better
for life after school. The design for the new school won the Civic Trust Environmental
Improvement Scheme Award and of the 796 UK entries, was the only one from Northern
Ireland. The judges remarked that the new buildings fitted in so well with the surroundings
and made use of the gardens and trees.[52]

The planning, design and construction of the school placed an enormous burden on
the board of governors and particularly on the headmistress. Mrs Norah Watts, the chairman
of the board, paid tribute to the tremendous role Miss Cunningham had played throughout
and underlined their indebtedness to her:

> But gathering all the threads together was the Headmistress. From the
> beginning Miss Cunningham strongly supported the Governors' decision
> to provide new buildings for the school and she has given her time and
> thought unsparingly to everything connected with them. Hers has been a
> most arduous and responsible task, and her name will always be associated
> with the removal of Victoria College . . . to Drumglass.[53]

Miss Cunningham and her staff at
the new school, 1972

'THE KING IS DEAD, LONG LIVE THE KING'[54]: CRANMORE PARK

No more we climb the attic stair
The school has moved this year;
But the old traditions of the past
Will still continue here.

We've spacious grounds and fine bright rooms
The furnishings are new;
We've playing fields and language labs.
A sixth-form centre too.

So old Victorians, parents, friends,
Come see our modern school;
And give us all the help you can,
To finish our swimming pool.

MARINA GIBSON[55]

In spring 1972 Victoria College moved from Lower Crescent to the grounds of Drumglass House and the school had a new address, Cranmore Park. The building was not yet complete but was sufficiently ready for the transfer. The process was far from smooth, for a two-day strike triggered by the prorogation of the Northern Ireland parliament left the school without heating or lighting and impeded removals. Miss Jeannie Hall, who was head of chemistry at the time, recalls that the ordeal was an 'utter nightmare', for the strikers prevented the removal vans from entering the car park at Drumglass. Inevitably, much was lost or mislaid in the transition, including a remarkable barometer from the physics laboratory, which had been used by students of the collegiate department in Dr Byers' day.[56]

The move was eventually completed, and while there was a wave of nostalgia for the old school, the benefits of the new building were greatly appreciated, particularly the space and the light and leafy surroundings. The peacefulness of the Cranmore site was a stark contrast to the noise of traffic and buzz of city life in Lower Crescent. At the first prize distribution in the new school Miss Cunningham declared that they were proud of and happy with their new building, and that the sixth formers were particularly delighted to have their own centre, complete with kitchen and lounge area. The new hall could easily accommodate all the pupils, but microphones were now needed in the assembly hall. Gym classes were a more carefree affair as the girls could now run freely without fear of splinters and examinations were no longer interrupted by the 'perpetual patter of rain drops falling into tin buckets'. Yet, for all its facilities, the new school lacked the character and the hustle and bustle of Lower Crescent.[57]

The new school was officially opened on 25 October 1972 by Lord Grey of Naunton, the last governor of Northern Ireland. There were various open days to enable parents and friends to tour the new buildings. In April 1973 a celebration ball was held to commemorate the move, but also, and importantly, to boost funds for the Development Fund. Some three hundred guests attended the occasion and enjoyed a candlelit dinner in the canteen and dancing in the hall.

Plans for the ring road were abandoned. The old school building was bought by the Belfast Corporation and later leased to, and subsequently bought by, the Crescent Youth Resource Centre, now the Crescent Arts Centre, which runs classes and workshops in all aspects of the arts. The building is undergoing a major refurbishment project and will reopen in March 2010.[58]

THE DEVELOPMENT FUND

In 1971 a development fund was started to supplement the grant from the Ministry of Education and to provide various amenities that were not covered by the subsidy, such as lighting for the stage, improvements to the boarding department and a swimming pool. The target was set at £75,000, but this later increased to £90,000. A series of parents' evenings was held to explain what was required and to encourage benefaction. This was the beginning of an arduous and protracted project that was hindered by inflation and also the Troubles, for riots, bomb scares and disruption to public transport deterred people from attending fundraising events and meetings. In 1979, thanks to the tremendous efforts of pupils, parents, staff, the OGA and the board of governors, the target was reached.

Money was raised through various events such as sales, concerts and sponsored swims, but after the initial surge of donations, progress was slow. A booster campaign was started in November 1975 and each pupil was asked to use her initiative to raise £5 for the appeal. One particularly enterprising pupil hit the headlines with her innovative scheme. Joanne Drew, who was a member of the North Down branch of the British Sub Aqua Club, decided to dive for coal in 'the murky depths of Bangor harbour'. She and her sister raised some 10cwt of coal, which they then sold to neighbours for £15.[59] The OGA produced a cookery book to augment the fund; this was initiated by the former head of Classics, Marjorie Moore, and was fittingly called *Mrs Moore's Cookbook*. A May fair was hosted by Mrs Bannie Bamford, vice president of the OGA, who was also the driving force behind the formation of a swimming club.

In January 1974 the seven-year-olds of P3 took the first plunge in the new pool. The official opening followed with a gala in March.[60] Pupils received instruction from Mrs Doreen Forsythe, and by the end of June there were few who could not swim a length of the pool. Families, friends and former pupils also had the opportunity to use the new facilities. A swimming club was established and lessons were offered to children and adults, a number of whom had grown up during the war and missed out on the opportunity to learn. They were now guided through their strokes by Mrs Forsythe. The pool has been a great asset to the school and has boosted the pupils' performance in swimming, life-saving and diving. Over the years pupils have achieved considerable success in both individual and team events; a number of girls have represented Ulster and Ireland, and several have distinguished themselves as British champions.

THE TROUBLES

We have learnt how to split the atom and walk on the moon since then [1921]
but seem to have made little progress in learning to live together in peace.
JOAN RUSSELL[61]

School life was inevitably affected by the Troubles, particularly when Victoria was situated in Lower Crescent. There were bomb scares, disruption to transport and the cessation of language exchange trips. Sports fixtures and events were frequently cancelled. In 1972, for example, the choir was unable to participate in any concerts outside school and there was even uncertainty as to whether examinations would go ahead.[62] Classes frequently finished early so that pupils might get home before public transport stopped running. Perhaps the most memorable incident during the Troubles occurred on 5 November 1970, when a hoax bomb scare at the school's annual prize distribution in the Whitla Hall meant that the entire assembly had to be evacuated into the pouring rain. The incident made the front page of the local press.[63] Throughout the Troubles, and despite the mayhem, the school never closed. When petrol was short staff would share lifts and, as Mary Boucher recalls, four or five teachers might squeeze in to one car. But everyone always managed to arrive for classes and for Margaret Andrews this was crucial, providing stability and continuity for the girls in chaotic times.

MISS CUNNINGHAM'S CLOSING YEARS

Schools may change in the years to come, but I hope that Victoria
College will retain its good name and will never lose sight of what I have
always considered to be its chief purpose, to send out into the world girls
who can appreciate beauty, truth and goodness; who can differentiate
between the significant and the insignificant, who have the will to serve
and the determination to live up to the best within themselves.
WEIR CUNNINGHAM[64]

Weir Cunningham brought Victoria College through difficult times and effectively 're-founded' it when she established the school at its new location in Cranmore Park. She was the longest-serving principal after Margaret Byers and, interestingly, also gave fifty-three years of service to the school, for she continued as president of the OGA for twenty-eight years after her retirement as headmistress. Her headship perhaps saw the most dramatic changes, with the transformation of a post-war society and the move from an old Victorian building in the centre of Belfast to a fully-equipped school in the leafy suburbs. Miss Cunningham respected tradition but, like her predecessors and successors, she believed in moving with the times and progressing the school. She also believed in trusting her pupils, as evidenced by the portrait that was unveiled in 1976. On this occasion Miss Cunningham pointed out that the artist, Tom Carr, had painted a figure of a pupil behind the headmistress, but she was not watching, as she trusted her girls.[65]

Miss Cunningham retired as headmistress of Victoria College in 1976 but retained an

Miss Cunningham's farewell dinner with staff and former members of staff, 1976

avid interest in the school and remained president of the OGA until her death in 2004. Miss Cunningham was no mere figurehead and played a pivotal role in the OGA – she was its very heart. In 2004, shortly before her death, Miss Cunningham celebrated her ninetieth birthday with a small luncheon party generously provided by Sir William Hastings; it was attended, fittingly, by her sister, nephew and members of the OGA. Even when her suffering was great, she retained the greatest affection for her former pupils and colleagues, whom she welcomed warmly:

> Her courage over those last few weeks was unbelievable. She received us with
> a big smile and open arms, 'Sit down and tell me all your news.' And we did,
> and she listened as she had always done.[66]

The Old Girls' Association, the FPA and *The Victorian* magazine

To unite Victorians in a common bond; to keep them in touch with their Alma Mater; and to provide opportunities for social intercourse
AIMS OF THE OLD GIRLS' ASSOCIATION

The Old Girls' Association (OGA) was officially constituted in 1915, with Miss Matier, the headmistress, as president and Miss Steele, English mistress, as secretary. The following year the OGA revived the school magazine, which it renamed *The Victorian*, and almost twenty years later, in 1935, members established the Victorians' Hockey Club. The club was opened to the public in the eighties; it continues to draw players from across Belfast and has a strong representation of former and current pupils and staff.

Initially the OGA comprised sixty-six members who met every January to enjoy an evening of conversation and entertainment hosted by Miss Matier. Later, the headmistress held several garden parties at Drumglass, where members played tennis and badminton. A second meeting was officially introduced in 1935 when a reunion was held in November at which the headmistress gave a brief report on the school; this practice continues today at the autumn reunion in October. As the OGA grew, it became customary for the January meeting to be a luncheon at a local hotel. In 1946 over one hundred members attended the New Year's luncheon at the Carlton restaurant, where the guest of honour was Mrs Grummit, chief commandant of the Girls' Training Corps, wife of the headmaster of the Royal Belfast Academical Institution and the parent of a boarder. Later it was usual for the January meeting to be held in the school lecture hall, where a roaring fire was lit to welcome members. Barbara Callender (née Lawson) recalls that prior to these reunions the pupils were instructed to leave the hall neat and tidy for the OGA, whom they regarded as 'a very special and powerful group'.[67]

Membership of the OGA rapidly grew and by 1945 had exceeded five hundred. At this time Winifred Templeton was honorary secretary, and she remained in office until her death in January 1977 when her assistant secretary, Betty Kerr, took over; between them, they have headed the association for over sixty-five years. Today the OGA is the largest in Ireland, with over one thousand five hundred members across the world; in fact the association is represented on every continent. Members are invited to attend three annual meetings – an autumn reunion, a dinner in spring and the AGM in October. Additional celebrations are held to commemorate anniversaries, retirements and other significant events. It is customary for the Association to present the school with a portrait of the headmistress upon her retirement and to commemorate the unveiling with a small reception.

Early beginnings: The FPA

While the OGA was formally constituted in 1915, its origins are in 1882, when the Former Pupils' Association (FPA) was formed. The FPA was begun by some of Mrs Byers' ex-pupils who wished 'to revive and perpetuate the pleasant memories of girlhood and to advance the development of the school'.[68] The group's main objective was to help promising students meet the costs of tertiary education, since no other funding was available to them in Belfast; this was not the case elsewhere in Ulster.[69] A scholarship committee was duly established and funds were administered by a group of seven men who acted as trustees. Money was secured from donors and through fundraising. An early benefactor was Mr John Shaw Brown, who in 1883 donated two annual scholarships, each of £20, with the proviso that his contribution should be matched by another source. This was generally achieved through the FPA's fundraising; they organised sales, cookery classes, lectures and concerts that might draw five hundred friends and supporters. One former pupil sought to spare the FPA the trouble of fundraising and donated money to establish the Ladies' Collegiate School Prize. This was to be awarded to any girl over eighteen years of age who could not afford to finance a university education, for the donor was particularly concerned to help young ladies who had to support themselves through industrial work.[70] By 1887 the FPA had raised £700 and was able to award eight scholarships tenable at Mrs Byers' collegiate department.

The restructuring of university education in the early twentieth century and the subsequent closure of Dr Byers' collegiate department in 1908 led to the disbandment of the FPA, which was no longer needed to support tertiary education at the school. The publication of the school magazine also ceased at this time, but was later rekindled by the OGA.

The Victorians' Hockey Club First Eleven, 1981–2, with their president, Professor Florence McKeown

The school magazine

The school must be primarily a place where a life is to be lived rather than where 'subjects' are to be taught. Where the average age of a generation is hardly more than five years the OGA offers a principle of integration and *The Victorian* records continuity of life.

ROSE MCLERNON[71]

The Ladies' Collegiate Magazine was launched in 1886 and was published three times a year. With the renaming of the school in 1887, it became known as *The Victoria College Magazine*. According to Mrs Byers, it was intended 'to retain the interest of former pupils' and offer 'a wider knowledge of women's education and other work'. Early editions had a light grey-blue jacket showing the Lower Crescent school on the front; from 1895 the cover was deep red and displayed the school badge. The magazine was essentially the joint work of students in the collegiate department and of members of the FPA. It included literary contributions, reports and news of former pupils, whether they were engaged in family life or religious and philanthropic work. But it was particularly concerned to report on 'the large band who have gone forth as teachers in secondary schools at home and in the colonies, and as missionaries from the various Protestant churches to foreign lands'.[72]

Production of the magazine ceased in 1906 but was revived ten years later by the newly formed OGA

and rebranded *The Victorian*. It gave news of former pupils, noted developments in the school and printed literary contributions from past and present pupils. The first magazine featured a magical Japanese tale, 'Métier de femme', by Helen Waddell, the renowned medievalist and a loyal Old Girl. It was reprinted in the magazine of 1937, 'lest latter-day wives should miss its message'.[73] Over the years there was some debate about content; a few claimed that contributions from Old Girls were 'intolerably long', while for others there was too much news about present pupils. In 1946 the editor, Dr Rose McLernon, responded to these complaints and conceded that although they could not 'win universal acclaim', they could and did provide a link between the past and the present.[74]

The OGA assumed responsibility for the editing and publication of the magazine until 1975, when it once more came under the school's auspices. Since then it has undergone various changes in colour, layout and design to reflect developments within the school, as well as advances in technology and printing. Following the amalgamation with Richmond Lodge School in 1987, the maroon jacket was replaced with a grey cover; in 1995–6 the A4-sized edition was launched. Now the maroon-covered magazine is an impressive panoply of colour photographs and reports which reflect the dynamic life of the school. With the advent of the internet, the magazine is now also available in electronic format on the school's website.

Continuity and change

Mrs Berner, Dr Higginson and the amalgamation with Richmond Lodge School, 1976–93

The school has a strong individuality shaped by the ideals enshrined in its founding aims. It has experienced a beneficial stability while showing a readiness to respond to changing circumstances.

GENERAL INSPECTION, 1985[1]

The annual preparatory school
Nativity play, 1984

In September 1985 a rigorous general inspection was conducted 'to gauge the quality of the learning experience offered to the pupil' at Victoria College. Over the course of a week representatives from the Department of Education (DENI) sat in on classes, shadowed specific forms, attended extracurricular activities and interviewed staff and pupils. They subsequently gave a positive appraisal and remarked on the 'well-maintained environment', the continuity in examination success and the 'excellent tone' of the school, which was built on its traditions but adapted to meet the needs of the time. Their report is a survey of the school as it was in 1985, in the aftermath of considerable upheaval in education, yet on the cusp of more significant and profound change with the reorganisation of the examination system, the introduction of a national curriculum and Victoria's amalgamation with Richmond Lodge School. But the report is also a testimony to the success of the principal, Mrs Brenda Berner, who had carried the school through challenging times and maintained continuity in the midst of immense change.

THE BERNER YEARS:
A WATERSHED IN EDUCATION

Everywhere one turns there is change; changes in the examination system, changes in subjects on the curriculum, changes of emphasis within subjects, changes arising from modern technology, changes in the conditions of service of teachers including the concept of the management of time, a change in the method of intake at the Transfer stage, a change in the allocation and management of resources in schools. One needs to be strong to survive it all.
BRENDA BERNER[2]

When Brenda Berner was appointed headmistress of Victoria College in 1976, it marked her return to the school, for as Brenda Kenyon she had been head girl of Victoria (1948–9), and also of its junior school at Strathearn (1945–6). Like her predecessor Miss Cunningham, Mrs Berner was a proficient linguist. She graduated from Queen's University Belfast in French and German and first taught at Coleraine High School. Mrs Berner was then head of modern languages at Strathearn School, where she was renowned as a brilliant and innovative teacher who pioneered a new method of language teaching in Northern Ireland; for two years her pupils heard only spoken French and the results were tremendous – 'fabulous accents [...] and an ability to think in French and respond spontaneously'.[3] Mrs Berner was principal of Cambridge House Girls' School in Ballymena for four years prior to taking up office at Victoria College.

Despite her many duties as headmistress, Mrs Berner initially retained her link with the classroom and taught both religious education and Italian, which she established as part of the school's curriculum. Moreover, she introduced the preparatory seven girls to French in their summer term. These lessons were eagerly anticipated by the girls and regarded as a highlight of the preparatory school experience. In addition to her abilities as a linguist and administrator, Mrs Berner was a distinguished fencer – an ex-internationalist and the first female advanced amateur coach. She instigated the formation of a fencing club at Victoria

Some of the first members of the school
fencing club, 1976–7

College, which has nurtured several Northern Ireland and British champions.

Mrs Berner was a respected figure in education in Northern Ireland and played an active role in the Ulster Headmistresses' Association and the Secondary Heads' Association. Towards the end of her headship she was faced with the momentous task of effecting the amalgamation of Victoria College with Richmond Lodge at a time of profound change in education.

EDUCATIONAL REFORMS

Change without improvement is a waste of time, energy and resources.
BRENDA BERNER[4]

The start of Mrs Berner's headship was dogged by the reorganisation of the selection procedure for eleven-year-olds and the imposition of tight pupil quotas by the Ministry of Education. Victoria College was fortunate to have the boarding department to accommodate extra numbers and Drumglass House was duly full. One positive outcome of the new system was the introduction of open days for prospective pupils and their parents, to help them make an informed decision about their choice of school.[5] But these were anxious times for Northern Ireland's grammar schools, whose very future was threatened by Labour's proposal to implement the comprehensive system of education, with schools for eleven- to sixteen-year-olds feeding sixth-form colleges. Their proposal generated considerable discussion and public debate and many feared comprehensive schooling would undermine Northern Ireland's system of education. Mrs Berner was concerned that it would deter pupils from continuing schooling after sixteen; those who did carry on would have to adjust to a new environment while preparing for important examinations. Not least, there was a real danger that good teachers would seek employment in the sixth-form colleges and be lost to younger pupils. She argued against 'change for change's sake and without improvement' and urged that they improve, rather than destroy a system that was 'known to work well'.[6] Objections were sent to Lord Melchett, Minister of State for Northern Ireland, but it was the election of Margaret Thatcher and the Conservative government in 1979 that brought an end to these plans and saved Northern Ireland's grammar schools.

This was a gloomy time for the profession and a difficult period for heads. Government cutbacks and the imposition of a reduced quota intake meant that there were fewer pupils, less income and staff shortages; as a consequence it was difficult to maintain the curriculum and any plans to build or upgrade the school's facilities had to be suspended. A growth in paperwork, numerous meetings and countless working parties took up an increasing amount of teachers' time and inevitably took them away from the classroom. These burdens and strains were exacerbated by the introduction of a new examination system and a national curriculum that was intended to revolutionise education. Teaching would now be centralised and pupils would learn through discovery rather than by rote; in effect, there was to be a new philosophy of teaching. While some welcomed the changes, others objected to standardisation and loss of teacher initiative and felt compelled to leave the profession. Victoria College had always prided itself on continuity of service, with many of its staff remaining at the school for most, if not all of their careers. Now, for the first time, teachers were resigning mid-year and without any alternative employment.[7]

Lisa Barros D'Sa (preparatory 1) makes
a presentation to Mrs Berner, 1978

AN EXPANDING CURRICULUM

Our aim is not merely to impart knowledge, but to make that knowledge relevant to tomorrow's situation and to help our pupils find a sense of social awareness and responsibility.

BRENDA BERNER[8]

Since its foundation in 1859, Victoria College has endeavoured to provide pupils with a liberal education to equip them for an ever-changing world. The curriculum continues to evolve in accordance with developments in the contemporary world. The high level of unemployment and the emergence of an increasingly competitive world in the 1980s instigated an extensive restructuring of the careers department. In 1986 timetabled classes were introduced in third form, while conferences, symposia and mock-interview evenings were organised for the sixth form. An important development at this time was the work-shadowing scheme, which provided members of sixth form with firsthand experience of the workplace. In 1995 this was extended to younger pupils with the introduction of the Take your Daughter to Work programme.[9] Careers education in Victoria continues to evolve to help pupils decide on a career and, crucially, to provide them with the necessary skills for life. It is now at the heart of the school curriculum.

The growing importance of and reliance on computers and technology has inevitably had a huge impact on the curriculum and, also, on the administration of the school. Victoria College has embraced technology to advance learning and administration and has been one of the first schools in Northern Ireland to adopt the pilot system of school timetable and record-keeping. Margaret Andrews, at that time a member of the teaching staff, was from the first convinced of the importance of computers in education, as a teaching tool and a subject, but also in administration. She initiated the introduction of computer studies to the school in 1983 and taught her first O-level class to a small group of dedicated sixth formers who met after school, since there was no timetabled slot available. They were among the first candidates in Northern Ireland to sit an O-level computer studies examination in June 1984. A computer club was formed to supplement learning in the classroom and there were plans to launch an A-level course. Progress was swift and by 1985 all classes received lessons in computer awareness. The school continues to advance with technology. With video-conferencing software, pupils can establish live links with schools in Belfast and farther afield, to 'share' classes and collaborate in projects. Victoria is currently engaged in an 'e-twinning' project with its partner school in Huelva, Spain, and will soon be able to communicate with pupils in Tanzania and Cameroon and acquire a greater understanding of their culture and environment. As Mrs Berner declared in 1987:

> In Victoria College we have always cherished our traditions but we
> have not allowed ourselves to be hidebound by them.[10]

The political scene has similarly shaped Victoria's curriculum. In 1988 Education for Mutual Understanding (EMU) was made statutory in schools, in an attempt to tackle problems of sectarianism and racism. By this time Victoria College already had a vibrant cross-community programme. Since 1983 pupils had participated in schemes such as PRISM (Peace and Reconciliation Inter-schools' Movement) and the City of Belfast Rambles. In 1985 the school forged an important link with Muckross Park College, Dublin, and began the Muckross Exchange, which continues to flourish. Over the years girls from both schools have enjoyed weekends of cultural and social activities in Belfast and Dublin; many friendships have been forged and numerous shopping trips taken. Following the formal introduction of EMU to the curriculum, additional cross-community links were established, including the junior and middle schools' partnerships with Dominican College, Fortwilliam, and Our Lady of Mercy Girls' Secondary School, Ballysillan; the boarding department's association with Rathmore School, Dublin; and the preparatory school's partnership with Our Lady's Primary School, Belfast. Through Co-operation Ireland's Civic Link programme, Victoria previously had a longstanding working relationship with St Louis' Community School in Kiltimagh, County Mayo and Lismore Comprehensive School in Craigavon. These associations have enabled pupils to share in many recreational activities and educational projects, including cultural outings, discussions and fundraising initiatives.

EXTRACURRICULAR ACTIVITIES

Perhaps the most significant contribution which a school makes to a
pupil's preparation for adult life occurs in encounters which take place
after or out of school.
JOY HIGGINSON[11]

Extracurricular activities play an increasingly vital role in education. They provide an opportunity to pursue interests, acquire new skills and work as a team. A number of these complement classroom teaching. Others are intended to meet current interests and trends and have included driving lessons and self-defence classes. The increasing importance of trade and industry in the eighties led to the establishment of a school bank run by the girls, for the girls.

In 1986 the mini-company scheme was launched for lower sixth pupils; it has since been renamed the Young Enterprise Scheme. Those who participate in this programme are offered a unique opportunity to form and run a company. They appoint a management committee, raise capital through selling shares and decide on a product which is then made, marketed and sold. Successful products produced by Victoria girls include Christmas cards, jewellery and a rather novel self-defence package. The scheme has expanded in recent years and the companies now sell their merchandise at craft fairs and in shopping centres.

Another valuable part of the school's extracurricular programme is the Duke of Edinburgh's Award scheme, which was introduced in 1977 by Dorothy Pendry, head of geography, and immediately generated an interest and enthusiasm. The scheme lapsed for several years but has been revived by Caroline Hart and is going from strength to strength. A significant number of pupils has participated in the scheme, with many completing all three levels. Some have had the opportunity to meet members of the royal family, and in February 1991 a pop group comprising five of Victoria's sixth-form pupils played for the Duke of Edinburgh at Hillsborough Castle.[12]

Extracurricular activities often provide an opportunity for collaboration with other

i

ii

i   Joanne Brown, staff pantomime,
December 2008

ii   Noel Spence and Kathleen Wood jive for
Children in Need, 19 November 1985

iii   Naomi McMurray, Heather Clark
and Helen Burn, staff pantomime,
December 2008

iii

schools. Victoria has always had strong links with RBAI, which has been considered its 'brother school' since Dr Byers' day when pupils would meet for social occasions hosted by their respective principals. In December 1979 the two schools embarked on a new venture and staged a joint play, *Under Milk Wood*. This was a great success and the first of many productions that have included operas and musicals. In November 1985 the choirs of RBAI and Victoria College joined with those of St Dominic's and St Malachy's, also in Belfast, to stage a spectacular performance of Andrew Lloyd-Webber's *Requiem*. The following year they performed *Carmina Burana*. The preparatory departments of Victoria College and RBAI (Inchmarlo) have also enjoyed collaborative projects and in 1998 a team comprising pupils from both schools won the Top of the Form Quiz, sponsored by the RUC.[13]

It was during Mrs Berner's headship that the Service of Nine Lessons and Carols was established. It was first held in December 1977 at Fisherwick Presbyterian Church and is regarded as a highlight of the school year. In 2006 the service was relocated to the splendid surroundings of St Anne's Cathedral. Another important annual event which started at this time is the school musical. The first, *West Side Story*, was staged in 1982; subsequent productions include *The Boyfriend*, *Oklahoma*, *Annie* and the memorable *Sound of Muscials* in 2008. While these were originally in-school productions, collaboration with other schools, chiefly St Malachy's and RBAI, has been usual in recent years.

Members of staff have always been willing to put their dignity and safety on the line for the sake of charity and entertainment. Over the years they have strutted down the catwalk for Comic Relief, jived for Children in Need and appeared pigtailed and freckled at staff–pupil hockey matches. Male members of staff have donned red suits and beards for Santa's grotto at the charity Christmas sale. The orderly queue of children waiting patiently to see Santa would invariably be mowed down by a stampede of senior girls when the word got out that Noel Spence or Stephen Doherty was this year's Father Christmas. While this practice has now lapsed, there are other opportunities for budding Santas. Each year Peter Wedderburn visits the nursery school in the guise of Father Christmas, while the boarders welcome a snowy-bearded Trevor McKee. Teachers have also joined the girls on gruelling challenges that include a trek around the Great Wall of China for Action Cancer and an ascent of Mount Kenya. One of the highlights of the school calendar is the annual staff pantomime, which has been written and directed by Carolyn Watson (née Weir) since its debut on the Victoria stage in December 1987. Carolyn, who is now head of the junior school, previously wrote productions for Richmond Lodge School. The 1987 performance, *Cinderella and the Forty Staff*, starred Lorraine Stanley as Cinderella, Peter Wedderburn as Prince Charming and Leah McCracken as the fairy godmother; as is customary, it incorporated scenes from the sixth-form formal within a version of Cinderella. But the pantomime is also an important fundraising event; the 2007 performance raised over £2,000 for charity.

SPORTS

When it came to athletics Mrs Morrison gave me every opportunity, support, encouragement and latitude, far above and beyond the call of duty. [...] Her support continued beyond my school days and throughout my athletic career and I cannot express what that meant to me at the time.

JANET BOYLE[14]

Sport continued to flourish and expand under the direction of Ann Morrison, head of PE. New sporting opportunities included golf, cross country, martial arts and table tennis. The latter proved extremely successful, and under the guidance of Stephen Doherty of the history department, Victoria College established itself as the premier team in Ulster. 1984 was a triumphant year and the school won all trophies and cups available. The tennis teams also had considerable success and dominated the Ulster schools' league in the late seventies, early eighties and also in the early nineties.

The school has a tradition of excellent jumpers, particularly high jumpers. Indeed, of the four Commonwealth Games medals that Northern Ireland has secured in the high jump, three were won by former pupils of Victoria College, namely Thelma Hopkins and Janet Boyle. Janet was a pupil at the school from 1975 until 1982 and returned as a member of the teaching staff for a brief spell in 1990. In 1986 she secured the bronze medal at the Commonwealth Games in Edinburgh and in 1990 took silver at Auckland; in 1988 she was placed twelfth in the Seoul Olympics, a remarkable achievement. Janet recalls the tremendous support and encouragement she received from both Ann Morrison and Mrs Berner. As a former sportswoman, Mrs Berner was supportive of her pupils' athletic endeavours and 'was wonderful' when Janet was selected for a prestigious training camp in Portugal shortly before her A-level examinations and faced the difficult decision of whether or not to accept. While Mrs Berner agreed with Janet's parents that her academic work might suffer as a consequence, she remarked that examinations could always be retaken but opportunities such as this came only once. Janet subsequently went to Portugal, which was a turning point in her athletic career, for there she realised just what she was capable of achieving. Janet retains a great respect for her headmistress, who offered such a balanced perspective at a defining moment. Janet's prowess in other school sports was, however, less remarkable. She claims that arms and legs would fly in all directions on the tennis court while there were casualties on the hockey pitch when she appeared brandishing her stick.[15] But, as Ann Morrison recalls, any sports day in which Janet was competing was very special; she felt tremendous pride when she turned on the television to watch the Seoul Olympics and saw Janet in action.[16]

THE AMALGAMATION:
THE BLENDING OF TWO TRADITIONS

In the blending of two very rich, similar and yet complementary traditions
we have a challenging opportunity to build up a school which will be positive,
forward-looking and stimulating.
BRENDA BERNER[17]

In February 1986 DENI first mooted the idea of amalgamation to Victoria College. The fall in school enrolments in south Belfast and the expectation that these would continue to drop meant that there were not enough pupils to provide the four girls' grammar schools with a minimum enrolment of five hundred. Two were to go. Princess Gardens and Ashleigh House duly combined to form a new school, Hunterhouse College, on the former Princess Gardens site. Victoria College and Richmond Lodge decided to build on their combined experiences and traditions to strengthen the amalgamated school.[18]

The speed at which amalgamation was to be effected was extraordinary, particularly in light of all the other changes that were to be implemented at this time, chiefly the introduction of GCSE examinations and the national curriculum, as well as new conditions of service for teachers. A merger of this kind is usually conducted over four years; here, it was concluded in less than two. The idea was first raised by DENI in February 1986, and eight months later they approved the development proposals drawn up by the boards of Victoria College and Richmond Lodge.

On 1 August 1987 the amalgamation was completed, with the school comprising a total of nine hundred pupils. The union was formally marked with a Service of Thanksgiving and Dedication in St Anne's Cathedral on 11 October 1987. This was an impressive and moving occasion. An academic procession of staff and clergy opened the proceedings; readings, prayers and music from the choir and orchestra followed. The soloist on this occasion, Giselle Allen, is now an internationally renowned opera singer. While new ties were forged, old ones were severed and the following year Strathearn School sought independence from Victoria College.

PREPARATION FOR AMALGAMATION

The planning and preparation for amalgamation were inevitably difficult for both schools. There were countless meetings and negotiations, and there were compromises to be made as

Third formers from Richmond Lodge and Victoria College who worked on a joint history project, with their teachers, Elisabeth Acheson (RL) and Stephen Doherty (VCB), 1986

the two heads, boards of governors and staff decided on how best to proceed, for they had not simply to integrate two schools, but had to operate on two sites. A series of joint events was arranged to ease the transition and provide an opportunity for pupils and parents to meet their counterparts. Highlights included a joint drama production, a wine and cheese evening organised by the Richmond Lodge Association of Teachers and Parents (ATP) and open days for parents and pupils to visit both sites. DENI accorded the schools several days of exceptional closure so that the staff from the two schools might meet to synchronise lessons, a difficult but crucial task if classes were to be successfully merged the following September. These, of course, were in addition to the many meetings and training days that teachers throughout Northern Ireland were required to attend to prepare for the imminent educational changes. It was therefore a particularly stressful time for the staff in both schools and, indeed, for their counterparts in Ashleigh House and Princess Gardens.

RESTRUCTURING THE SCHOOL

The relative strengths of the two schools placed Victoria College in the position of 'senior partner' in recognition of which the name 'Victoria College' is to continue. However, the name of Richmond Lodge will not be lost either – a new House is to be called Richmond House; the brand new library […] will be the Richmond Lodge Library; and the words 'incorporating Richmond Lodge School' are to appear on headed notepaper, correspondence issued to parents and on school reports.

JOAN RUSSELL[19]

The amalgamated school retained the name Victoria College and remained under the headship of Mrs Brenda Berner. Dr Joy Higginson, the headmistress of Richmond Lodge, officiated as deputy headmistress, and Margaret Andrews became vice principal. Additional posts were created to deal with the complexity of administering a larger school. Four members of senior staff, Austin Gibson, Jeannie Hall, Leah McCracken and Patricia Pyne, were appointed and made responsible for specific aspects of the school, such as examinations and the sixth form. Year heads and sixth-form tutors were introduced to help with welfare, both academic and pastoral. The Victoria College board of governors was extended to include nine Richmond Lodge board members, but it remained under the chairmanship of Mrs Joan Russell.

The amalgamated school was to operate from two campuses, with a junior school comprising years eight to ten on the Richmond site and the senior school on Victoria's Cranmore campus. The preparatory department was located at Cranmore and a new playgroup and reception class opened in the Garden Room on the Richmond site. This has been a wonderful asset and continues to flourish under the direction of Catherine Chambers.

To acknowledge and represent the amalgamation, the Victoria College coat of arms was modified to incorporate the galleon of Richmond Lodge School, and a new uniform was designed. The girls were allowed to wear out their existing uniforms and there was initially a great variety of combinations and styles of dress. In the first year of the amalgamation the head girls and deputies of both schools officiated, but since then one head girl and two deputies are elected and supported by the Sixth-form Council, or Senior Council as it is now known. In 1997 the prefect system was reintroduced and some thirty-five prefects form the Senior Council. Examination classes were not merged in the first year of amalgamation but continued in the same groupings and with the same teachers to minimise disruption. This applied to fifth formers, who were the first GCSE candidates, the upper-sixth A-level classes and the P7 pupils who were sitting the qualifying examination.

The amalgamation was not without its difficulties. While Mrs Berner remarked on its success and the relative smoothness of the transition, she conceded that the first year had been challenging, 'characterised by unremitting labour and relentless pressure in a constant race against time'.[20] Much of the burden was shouldered by the staff, for in the first year each taught on both campuses to establish unity and cohesion. This added to the complexity of timetabling, which required that teaching was coordinated on two sites, that staff had time to commute and that examination classes retained their teachers. The Herculean task of timetabling was accomplished by Margaret Andrews, Leah McCracken, Austin Gibson and Trevor Grattan, and many packets of Polo mints were devoured in the process!

The split site posed more potential problems. There was a danger that the younger pupils would feel isolated and removed from the main hub of college life, but under the strong guidance of Kate Lawton, head of junior school and an old girl of Richmond Lodge, a strong system of pastoral support was established and links were formed between the two campuses. The senior girls frequently visited the junior site in their capacity as form helpers, and to lead societies and run the school bank. A Junior School Council was established to provide the younger girls with a forum to air their views, and a Middle School Council was formed thereafter.

While the mechanics of operating two campuses were not always easy, there were benefits. This was apparent in December 1987 when a bomb exploded in Cadogan Park, causing damage to the main building on the Richmond site. The junior school girls were evacuated to the Cranmore campus, where they were helped by the senior girls; as head girl Karen Irwin remarked, 'the spirit of cooperation and goodwill was never more in evidence'.[21]

Despite all the upheaval, the examination results were good, particularly in the new GCSE examinations. Moreover, there were visible benefits of having a larger school. With more staff and facilities, Victoria College could support a wider curriculum and offer pupils a greater choice with new subjects such as politics and drama. Setting replaced streaming in English, mathematics and French, so that each girl could be placed in a class that best suited her needs and ability. Not least, the school could draw on two traditions to enrich the education it offered girls both within and outside the curriculum. For example, the Richmond Lodge tradition of Festival has been retained in the junior school. Once a fortnight, all the pupils share an activity: they might have a visiting speaker, participate in a quiz or perform a play. For many years, the highlight of Festival was the annual Shakespeare competition, an event which owed much to the energy and creativity of Kate Lawton, who 'was the driving force' behind this.[22] The House system that has operated in Victoria College since 1936 similarly encourages forms to cooperate and collaborate in a friendly spirit of competition.

In 1989 Mrs Berner retired from the school. This was particularly sad for girls in the lower sixth who had started at the preparatory school on Mrs Berner's first day as headmistress.

They included Noelle Hall (née Pierce), who was deputy head girl in 1989–90. Noelle recalls Mrs Berner's final assembly in June 1989 when she, along with Debbie Cochrane (née Hewitt), the head girl, and Alison Phillips (née Cooley), the other deputy, presented the headmistress with a set of garden furniture on behalf of the girls. This had been hastily put together on the stage, which 'resembled a set from *Sale of the Century*'. When a delighted Mrs Berner invited the girls to join her on the swing-chair, any twinges of sadness Noelle may have felt were rapidly replaced by fears for the principal's safety; Noelle had visions of the entire set collapsing on the stage and before the whole school.[23] Fortunately, the bolts held and an accident was averted, but it was a memorable occasion.

Astute, clear-thinking and with an enormous capacity for work, Mrs Berner is remembered as 'an excellent administrator' who, as Patricia Pyne explains, remained 'calm under pressure' and had an 'ability to resolve a never-ending stream of matters that arose before, during and after amalgamation'.[24]

DR JOY HIGGINSON 1989–93: ARTICULATE, WITTY AND COMPASSIONATE

We try to create … a school environment in which the pursuit of
excellence is respected, achievement is applauded and each individual
is loved for what she is irrespective of what she achieves.
JOY HIGGINSON, 1991[25]

Dr Joy Higginson succeeded Mrs Berner as principal of Victoria College in 1989. She read English language and literature at Queen's University Belfast, and then embarked on a rich and varied teaching career that began at a diocesan boarding school in Jamaica, continued in Northern Ireland (Wallace High School, Lisburn, and Ashleigh House), progressed through England (Brighton Polytechnic) and Scotland (Albyn School, Aberdeen), and ended once more in Northern Ireland, when she returned as headmistress of Richmond Lodge School in 1985. In the same year she received her doctorate from the University of Sussex.

Following the merger with Victoria College, Dr Higginson officiated as deputy head for two years before her appointment as principal. At this time Victoria was still a newly amalgamated school and in the throes of establishing the national curriculum; it was thus acclimatising to fresh demands and grappling with a new language as terms such as 'key stage' and 'league tables' became everyday parlance. There were major building projects to undertake to equip the school for the new curriculum, and a fundraising campaign was begun to support this work. The Development Fund was started and completed within the four years of Dr Higginson's headship, and was largely achieved through her 'energy and commitment'.[26]

THE DEVELOPMENT FUND

The Development Fund was launched in January 1990, with a target of £500,000, to subsidise and boost DENI's grant aid and provide the school with the necessary facilities to meet the needs of a changing curriculum. Projects included the building of a new library and of a technology

Dramatic architecture, the
Richmond Lodge Library

and design centre for each campus, and improvements to sport and media facilities. By May 1990 over £400,000 had been raised through the efforts and generosity of the Association of Parents and Teachers (APT), staff, governors and former pupils.[27]

On 7 November 1990 the library and resource centre, known as the Richmond Lodge Library, was formally opened by HRH the Duchess of Gloucester, 'who ran far behind her schedule in her determination to meet everyone and see every exhibit'.[28] This impressive building comprises an audio-visual room and computer suite, in addition to the library itself. It commemorates Richmond Lodge School, whose motto, 'The gateway to knowledge is humility', welcomes pupils entering the library. The opening of the Technology and Design Centre followed on 21 February 1992. This ceremony was performed by Dr Sarah Springman, fellow of Magdalene College, Cambridge, engineer and national triathlete champion, who delighted her audience by addressing them in English and French.[29]

In 1993 Victoria College was 'in the vanguard of progress' once more and became the first school in Northern Ireland to have its own AstroTurf tennis courts. At the opening of the courts in June 1993, three exhibition matches were played by the school's junior and senior teams. A third team comprised four former pupils who had distinguished themselves in the sport, namely, Natalie Patterson (née Moffett) and Julie Maguire (née Hastings), who have both played for Ulster, and Dianne Mayne (née Craig) and Claire Curran, who have represented Ireland. Claire subsequently enjoyed a six-year professional career in the sport, winning twelve International Tennis Federation doubles titles. In 1997 a new modern languages building was finished. The next major challenge is the redevelopment of the Cranmore campus, so that the entire school can be accommodated on one site.

RETIREMENT

A lady of quick observation and ready wit, she had the ability to deliver
a thought-provoking sermon in morning assembly or tell a good story
at a staff social occasion.
ANNE MCBRIDE AND PATRICIA PYNE[30]

Dr Higginson retired in 1993 owing to ill-health. While her headship was relatively short, she achieved much, and not only carried the Development Fund to its completion – a tremendous achievement – but made an important and enduring impact on the spirit of the school. Dr Higginson insisted on consideration for others. This extended to the school buildings and grounds, which were to be kept litter-free and tidy. Thanks to the tremendous efforts (and vigilance) of the headmistress and her vice principal, Austin Gibson, Victoria College won the award for the Best Kept Large School in Belfast in 1993. A standard was set and the school has frequently been the recipient of this award since, remaining committed to preserving a clean and eco-friendly school.[31] It was also during Dr Higginson's headship that the management committee decided to hold a special Christmas reception for last year's school leavers, as many girls now attended universities and institutions on the UK mainland and were unable to be present at their final prize day. This has become an annual fixture in the school calendar and is an important way of maintaining ties.

Dr Joy Higginson, 1993

Articulate, witty and quick-thinking, Dr Higginson had the gift 'to defuse any situation with an apt quotation or anecdote'.[32] Her office door was open to staff and pupils alike, and she was always generous with her time and ready with her praise. Above all she will be remembered for her humility and compassion, and her endeavours to strengthen the school as a unified community.

THE GATEWAY TO KNOWLEDGE IS HUMILITY

Richmond Lodge School

Richmond Lodge School has its origins around 1879 when three daughters of a linen merchant, the Misses Jessie, Florence and Lucy Hardy, opened a preparatory school for boys 'and rather grudgingly admitted several of their sisters'. However, it was the arrival of Miss Violet Nairn in 1911 that marks its real beginnings, for it was she who named the school Richmond Lodge, resettled it on the Malone Road and shaped the school's identity. Accordingly, her headship is considered the formative period in Richmond Lodge's history: in 1961 the Old Girls (the Arellians) celebrated the fiftieth anniversary of her arrival.[33]

Early beginnings:
'a dame school with a difference'[34]

It is not known where exactly the three Misses Hardy opened their school, but by 1884 they were established at 28 Elmwood Avenue in south Belfast. All classes were held in the one room. In 1890 they relocated to more spacious premises at 13 Stranmillis Road, which was later the studio of the artist, William Conor, and is now a restaurant. The ladies lived next door to the school along with their brother. At this time the school was primarily for boys, most of whom progressed to boarding school in England. The three sisters shared the teaching, but there was no timetable as such and, as Nesca Robb explains, 'classes took place as and when circumstances and Miss Jessie's convenience permitted'.[35]

In 1903 Miss Sarah Garrett took over the reins. Prior to her appointment she had been a member of Mrs Byers' teaching staff at Victoria College and this experience influenced her restructuring of the Hardys' school, which under her headship became primarily for girls and was renamed accordingly the Ladies' Preparatory School. Miss Garrett sought to provide pupils with a liberal education within a structured timetable. Mistresses were engaged to teach by subject and classes were given in drama, drill, singing, dancing and deportment. A literary society was begun. In 1911

Miss Garrett left the school for health reasons and was succeeded by Miss Violet Nairn whose sister, Edith, was the dance teacher.

The formative years

The arrival of Miss Violet Nairn heralded a new stage in the school's history. In 1912 she acquired Rupert Lodge on the Malone Road, which was previously known as Richmond House and later as Grey House. This became 'the heart and soul of the school' for many generations of pupils and the building is now, fittingly, called Nairn House. Miss Nairn admitted a small number of senior girls and renamed the school Richmond Lodge High School for Girls to reflect changes in its location and make up. Soon thereafter Miss Nairn introduced the distinctive school colours, 'saxe and black', and adopted a school song and motto, 'The gateway to knowledge is humility'. The galleon was taken on as the badge of Richmond Lodge. Throughout its history, these have remained the hallmarks of the school.

Miss Nairn gave Richmond Lodge its character and ethos. Classes were conducted in a relaxed teaching environment, to promote freedom of thought and a community atmosphere. 'Festival' was introduced to encourage girls of all ages to work together. The Intermediate Examinations had not been an issue for the school until the admission of senior girls in 1912, but then, as Nesca Robb explains, they 'were not so much as named among us', for Miss Nairn believed that work should be its own reward and was vehemently opposed to public examinations.[36] However, as a consequence of the Education Act of 1923, the school had to reconsider its position to qualify for state help.

Richmond Lodge was distinctive not only in its attitude to work, but to sport, for the girls played lacrosse

The Richmond Lodge lacrosse team

rather than hockey. Indeed, for many years it was the only lacrosse-playing school in Ireland.[37] Richmond Lodge promoted the Girl Guide movement in Ulster and was a pioneer of Guide camps. The Richmond Lodge Guide Company (the 2nd Belfast), which was formed in 1914, was the first school company in Ulster. It continues to thrive and is now the oldest company in Ulster with an unbroken record.

Miss Nairn stamped her imprint on the school and imbued it with an individuality. She resigned from the headship in 1920 and was replaced by Miss Amy Purvis, who had been one of the first to qualify from Mrs Byers' Froebel Department. Her headship saw considerable changes to the structure of the school. A board of governors was constituted, pupils were required to enter public examinations and a uniform was introduced. The Old Girls' Association (the Arellians) was established in 1917, a small secretarial department was opened in 1939 and the Parents' Association was formed in 1945. Additional buildings were acquired to accommodate the growing numbers, but the school retained its 'friendly atmosphere' and 'quietly flourished'.[38]

Members of the 2nd Belfast Guide Company enjoying camping

Richmond Lodge School *c.*1944;
headmistress Miss Amy F. Purvis
is pictured with members of staff
and pupils

Richmond Lodge following the war

*Life went on at an accelerated pace when she was
around, for she was rapid in everything she did.*
NESCA ROBB[39]

In 1946 Miss Elizabeth Maxwell was appointed
headmistress of Richmond Lodge and was to lead the
school for over twenty years. She was a distinguished
English graduate of Queen's University Belfast,
having obtained a First Class Honours degree. Miss
Maxwell was witty, sharp and incisive; she had a strong
personality but was greatly loved and respected. She
contributed much to the spirit of Richmond Lodge
and led the way in forging partnerships with other
schools and fostering international links. Under
Miss Maxwell's guidance Richmond Lodge became
a leading proponent of the Council for Education
in World Citizenship (CEWC). Both Victoria College
and Richmond Lodge were founding members of the
Belfast Schools' World Citizenship Association; indeed,
the first meeting in November 1948 was held in Lower
Crescent, and the third in Richmond.[40] Whereas
enthusiasm for this in Victoria College had waned by
1967, Richmond Lodge remained a leading light and
since the amalgamation of the schools in 1987, CEWC

has been a vibrant and integral part of the school's
extracurricular activities. Following the death of Miss
Maxwell in 2000, the Arellians presented the Maxwell
Award for World Citizenship to the school as a tribute
to her work.[41]

Miss Maxwell's headship also saw changes
to the status and structure of Richmond Lodge. In
1947 it became a voluntary B grammar school and
remained so until 1961 when essential building work
required the school to alter its status to qualify for
a government subsidy. Richmond duly became a
voluntary A school and construction began on a new,
modern building. This was opened in November 1966
by the scientist, Dame Honor Fell.

Miss Maxwell retired in 1967 and was followed
in the post by her vice principal, Miss Christine
Campbell who, in 1972, was succeeded by her vice
principal, Mrs Elizabeth Armstrong. Joan Cupitt, who
was a young teacher in the preparatory department
during Mrs Armstrong's headship, recalls that she
was helpful and warm and always ready to offer
advice.[42] In 1985 Mrs Armstrong was succeeded by
Dr Joy Higginson, who led the school through the
amalgamation with Victoria College, where she was
deputy principal and later headmistress.

Progressing onward

Mrs Andrews, Ms Slevin and a new millennium

Times have changed certainly, but Victoria
has changed in accordance.

JOAN RUSSELL[1]

Ms Slevin with the principals, staff and pupils of
the Royal Bilingual College and Star Bilingual
School, Doualain; Mr Scott Naismith, principal
of Methodist College; and Mr Alan Jennings,
principal of Downey House, to initiate the
Connecting Classrooms Project, April 2009

Implementation of the national curriculum and the compilation of league tables heralded a new era in education, with an increasing emphasis on skills, values and citizenship alongside content. Careers education is now at the core of the curriculum, while advances in technology and communication mean that opportunities both within and outside the classroom are rich and varied. Pupils can forge global links and communicate in real time with schools across the world. They engage in political debates, participate in model UN General Assemblies and meet diplomats. They can learn Chinese and sign language and embark on extreme challenges such as climbing Mount Kilimanjaro. Yet the ethos of the school has remained constant. Throughout its 150-year history, Victoria College has endeavoured to provide pupils with a liberal education, to offer them every opportunity available and to keep abreast of new developments. Mrs Margaret Andrews and Ms Patricia Slevin have led Victoria through these changing times and into a new millennium. They have built on the traditions of both Victoria College and Richmond Lodge to equip pupils for the future and enable them to reach their full potential.

MRS MARGARET ANDREWS: LEADING A LEADER

Her leadership skills are second to none and she has taken great pride in ensuring that in Victoria College not only the pupils but each of the staff is stretched and challenged [...] She never allows herself – or any of us – to become complacent. There's always something more, some new challenge to be faced, another pilot, another initiative, another opportunity to go a bit further, to reach for the sky.

PATRICIA SLEVIN[2]

In 1971 Margaret Andrews joined the teaching staff of Victoria College in Lower Crescent. She was then Miss Meenan, but after the Easter holidays returned to the new building in Cranmore Park as Mrs Andrews. This was her first post after graduating from Queen's University Belfast with a First Class Honours degree in mathematics, and she remained at Victoria College for her entire teaching career. Miss Cunningham, who had appointed Mrs Andrews to the staff, was immensely proud that it was she who had brought her into the school. Both Mrs Andrews and Mrs Faris were graduates in mathematics and shared the rather unusual experience of each being headmistress and a school parent. This gave them a unique insight into the school and its pupils.

Indeed, Mrs Andrews experienced Victoria from almost every perspective, first as a junior mistress, then as head of department (1984–6), senior teacher (1986–7), vice principal (1987–9), deputy head (1989–93) and, finally, headmistress (1993–2005). Accordingly, when she was appointed headmistress in 1993 Mrs Andrews had an acute understanding of the organisation of the school, a sympathy with the staff and personal experience of the problems and concerns facing parents and pupils. Moreover, years of timetabling the classes – a real exercise in people management – meant that she really knew her staff. Timetabling was a task that Mrs Andrews adored and was reluctant to give up. She continued it for the first years of

Mrs Margaret Andrews, 2005

her headship and would often become so immersed in the task that her husband, Ronnie, would have to tap the office window late at night to prise her away from the computer.[3]

Former pupils remember Mrs Andrews as a dedicated and passionate teacher who enthused and enthralled. One such devotee is Noelle Hall (née Pierce), who was inspired to become a mathematics teacher. She recalls the tremendous energy with which Mrs Andrews conducted her classes; they were dynamic from start to finish. Mrs Andrews would enter the room at great speed and write vigorously on the blackboard, creating a cloud of chalk dust. As her rapture grew, the hands moved ever more frantically through her hair, and by the end of the lesson the girls beheld a chalk-faced and chalk-haired teacher.[4]

This passion and dedication also defined her headship. Mrs Andrews considered it her task to ensure that each pupil and member of staff reached his or her full potential and received the necessary support and encouragement to do so. Despite the growing pressure of meetings and paperwork, she participated in school trips and partnerships with other institutions, and remained involved in every aspect of college life. Mrs Andrews knew and was known to all her pupils, from the preparatory department to the senior classes. It was thus fitting that the tributes to mark her retirement were personal and warm. At the school's annual spring concert in 2005, the choir performed a piece commissioned to commemorate her retirement, 'A new tomorrow', and a preparatory-school girl composed a poem in honour of a much-loved headmistress:

> Encourages us all,
> Nice clothes, rather tall.
>
> Watches us at Prize Day, loves the show
> Oh, Mrs Andrews, do you have to go?
>
> We will remember her, she is great,
> She is the one we ALL appreciate.
> MADIE CARWILE[5]

Margaret Andrews served as a member of the senate of Queen's University Belfast from 1998 to 2006, and in 2004 she was awarded the OBE in recognition of her services to education. She still retains a keen interest in the school and as president of the OGA is 'a tower of strength' to the office-bearers and committee.[6]

The annual Teddy Bears' picnic, 2002: a highlight of the preparatory school experience

Ms Patricia Slevin, 2005

MS PATRICIA SLEVIN:
'OPTIMISTIC, ENTHUSIASTIC AND DETERMINED'[7]

An energetic, innovative and dedicated leader […] She sets high
expectations for pupils and staff in all aspects of school life whilst the
combination of optimism, hard work, dignity and sense of humour make
her an excellent role model for future generations.

HILARY WOODS[8]

In 2005 Ms Patricia Slevin, who had officiated as vice principal of Victoria College since 2000,
succeeded Mrs Andrews as headmistress. She is a graduate of Queen's University Belfast in
French language and literature. Prior to her arrival as a teacher of English and French at
Victoria College, Ms Slevin taught at St Ciaran's High School, Ballygawley, and St Patrick's
Girls' Academy, Dungannon. She then worked as a field officer in modern languages for the
Belfast Education and Library Board. When Ms Slevin joined the teaching staff at Victoria in
1994, she became the link teacher for the Council for Education in World Citizenship (CEWC).
In this capacity, and as a teacher of the European studies course, she has liaised with schools
across Europe to initiate projects and partnerships, thereby establishing Victoria as a truly
international school.

Ms Slevin gained great popularity as a teacher at Victoria and was known not only to
those whom she taught, but to the large number of girls she accompanied on school trips and

with whom she engaged in projects. According to one former pupil, Ms Slevin was always a strong presence in the school, not least in the corridors where she would make it her business to learn girls' names, whether to offer a greeting or issue a reprimand.[9] As headmistress, she is greatly admired by the pupils and staff for her strength, independence and warmth. One preparatory school pupil who was asked about her headmistress simply replied that Ms Slevin visits their assembly every week, 'always with a big smile'.[10] Ms Slevin remains actively involved in the girls' projects and activities and had even intended to accompany two sixth-form pupils on a charity trek along the Great Wall of China. Unfortunately, a serious car crash in March 2006 prevented her from doing so. Still, she significantly boosted the girls' fundraising efforts by securing a signed guitar from the rock band Snow Patrol. A wonderful testimony to the great affection the girls have for their headmistress is the magnificent reception they gave her at their final assembly of the academic year in June 2006. Ms Slevin was on sick leave to recover from her injuries, but returned to wish the girls a good holiday and was greeted by a spontaneous standing ovation and cheers.[11]

AN INTEGRATED AND INCLUSIVE COMMUNITY

A community in which everyone has a place, everyone has responsibility,
one for the other, helping and supporting each other along the path of knowledge.
MARGARET ANDREWS[12]

The ethos of Victoria College is exemplified by the millennium statue, 'To lead a leader', which was presented to the school by the Association of Parents and Teachers (APT) and the Old Girls' Association (OGA). Victoria College is an integrated and inclusive community, and it fosters an environment where both pupils and staff are supported and encouraged to realise their potential. The school is fortunate to have dedicated teachers who are committed to advancing education for girls and meeting the needs of each pupil. Indeed, on hearing that only one girl wished to take A-level Italian, Linda Diffin responded immediately that all she needed was one pupil who wished to learn. She would gladly teach the course after school if there was no available slot in the timetable.

The compassion of the teachers and their concern for pupils' welfare has nurtured a strong school community. This is particularly important at times of loss and sorrow and no more so than in 2006–7. This was a difficult year for Victoria College. In March 2006 Ms Slevin was badly injured in a car crash. That December the school was stunned and deeply shocked when a popular and well-loved sixth former, Jane McVeigh, died suddenly from a severe allergic reaction. The girls were distraught but the support they received was absolutely marvellous and, as a former pupil, Hannah Lyons, recalls, the members of staff were wonderful. All classes were stopped on the day the news was broken and the teachers gathered the girls in the sixth-form centre, where they gave them tea and offered consolation. The pupils drew great comfort from this solidarity and support. Shortly thereafter, in February 2007, the school mourned another death when a member of the junior school, Sarah Barr, lost her battle with cancer; this was particularly upsetting as she was the daughter of the much-loved deputy head. There was a lot of grief and sadness at this time, but what stands out most for

'To lead a leader', the millennium statue

Hannah was the appearance of her headmistress on the day that the girls heard of Jane's death. Ms Slevin was herself recovering from injuries and was clearly in severe pain. Yet, showing dignity and strength, she walked into the assembly hall and addressed the girls. She drew the school together, and this is what they needed. They took great strength from her example, and for many this will be the greatest lesson and most enduring memory of their schooldays.[13]

There are various positive ways in which the school community responds to such tragedies. Former colleagues and friends are commemorated through the establishment of prizes in their name, the presentation of a work of art in their memory or the planting of a tree in their honour. In 2000 a special Millennium Garden was created in the school grounds, where staff, pupils and parents planted bulbs and shrubs to remember loved ones.[14] Here also is the statue, 'Young Forever', which was presented to the College by the family of Jane McVeigh. The school also supports relevant charities connected with former friends. Following the deaths of Sarah and Jane, the girls raised money to support the Anaphylaxis Campaign and the Northern Ireland Cancer Fund for Children. Both Richmond Lodge and Victoria College have a long tradition of fundraising for charity and of helping voluntary services at home and abroad. This work continues today. In recent years pupils have responded to international crises such as the Boxing Day tsunami in the Indian Ocean in 2004. The Senior Council held a non-uniform day to raise money for a fishing boat for a Sri Lankan village. In March 2005 pupils collaborated with members of staff to organise a community breakfast in aid of the Sudan crisis. The girls also raise money to augment school funds and, particularly,

Pupils and staff who ran the marathon for the Anaphylaxis Campaign, May 2007

to subsidise the sixth-form formal, which remains a highlight of their social calendar.

With tighter budgets and a greater demand for facilities, schools are now more reliant than ever on voluntary support. Victoria College is greatly helped by the APT, which holds several fundraising events throughout the year. They include a craft fair, a second-hand uniform sale and a spring ball. All proceeds are given to the school. The Victoria College APT is a continuation of the Parents' Association begun in 1945 by Miss Purvis and the parents of Richmond Lodge pupils. It remains an important part of the wider school community.

A CHANGING EDUCATION

Academic excellence is ensuring that no matter what talents or abilities
a child has they are developed to their full potential.
MARGARET ANDREWS, 2004[15]

Since 1989 education in Northern Ireland has undergone considerable change, and it is still evolving with the implementation of revised curricula and the introduction of new courses. These include learning for life and work, theatre studies and law. In 2000 AS-level examinations were introduced for Year 13 pupils, to broaden the curriculum and avoid specialism. However, they have greatly increased the pressure on pupils and teachers who are literally on 'a public examination conveyor belt'.[16] In spite of this Year 13 pupils continue to explore more vocational and practical activities, such as digital photography, Young Enterprise and European Studies. Learning opportunities are enhanced through collaboration with other schools and Victoria is an active member of the South Belfast Area Learning Community.

Education in Northern Ireland continues to evolve. But a lack of clarity as to the nature of forthcoming change means that it is often difficult for schools to anticipate and prepare for what lies ahead. Recent and radical change to the transfer system in Northern Ireland has caused great uncertainty. Selective transfer for eleven-year-olds has generated controversy and debate since its introduction in 1947. Most have agreed that the system is unsatisfactory, but as yet no better alternative has been produced. From 2010 the Department of Education will no longer provide a transfer test for eleven-year-olds. Victoria College and other grammar schools wishing to retain academic selection are planning to set entrance tests in a deregulated system. The political disunity over future education policy and particularly the transfer system means that this is a difficult and anxious time for Northern Ireland's schools. A great strength of Victoria College is the fact that it educates pupils from three to eighteen years of age, thus ensuring continuity in learning. Teachers in the secondary school are in touch with educational developments at primary and preparatory level, and are familiar with the abilities of pupils entering the senior school in Year 8. This is especially valuable given the current state of volatility within the system.

Dr Byers believed that girls were worthy of an education equal to that of boys and was determined that her school should provide them with such. It is fitting that in its sesquicentennial year, Victoria College has distinguished itself nationally in engineering and science. In January 2009 the school team triumphed in the United Kingdom final of a prestigious engineering competition that required entrants to design and build a carbon dioxide-powered GT racing car. Victoria College has gained recognition as a specialist school for science . It thus continues to advance its reputation as a progressive school for girls.

AN INTERNATIONAL SCHOOL

We will continue to work through partnerships with parents, governors
and the local and global community, to promote academic excellence and
to nurture innovation and creativity in a progressive and caring community.
PATRICIA SLEVIN[17]

Victoria College is recognised as an international school and has been accorded the British Council International School Award. Through its curricular and extracurricular activities, the school has created a rich and dynamic cultural learning experience. Pupils and staff have forged partnerships with schools and institutions throughout Europe and welcome visitors from across the globe. These have included a party of delegates from the United States of America and a group of schoolgirls from Durban College, South Africa. A number of exchange programmes is run for groups and individuals. For example, since 1991 pupils from Victoria College and the Royal Belfast Academical Institution have participated in exchange trips with the Ratsgymnasium Stadthagen, near Hanover, which affords an opportunity to experience school and family life in another country. Staff also benefit from exchange schemes. In September 2001 Dave Conarroe from Aspen High School, Colorado, exchanged with Ernie Thompson of Victoria College for a year through the Fulbright Exchange Programme. The chance to teach under a different system of education was insightful for both men, but the exchange was also culturally beneficial for the host schools and cemented the ties between them. Thus in June 2005 Dave Conarroe returned to visit Victoria with a team of basketball players from Aspen High School.[18]

Richmond Lodge and Victoria College have always forged strong international links. Indeed, Miss Elizabeth Maxwell OBE, headmistress of Richmond Lodge from 1946 to 1967, was a member of a UNESCO committee, 'a pioneer of cross-community projects' and a leading proponent of CEWC.[19] In more recent years, the school's international dimension has been greatly enhanced by Ms Slevin's involvement with the Comenius Project. This EU programme is sponsored by the British Council and provides a forum for teachers and pupils across Europe to learn with and from each other, and to augment education in their respective schools. Ms Slevin has initiated two major Comenius School Development Projects to anticipate and support changes in the curriculum. From 2002 to 2005 she led Victoria into partnerships with schools in Germany, Italy, Malta and Ireland, who together embarked on the Active Citizenship Programme. This was followed by a three-year project, Fit for Life, with schools in Germany, Poland and Sweden, helping pupils make informed choices about their careers. Ms Slevin continues to advance the school's international identity and is currently working with Methodist College to establish partnerships in sub-Saharan Africa while a new Comenius school project is being developed with schools in Estonia, Germany, Italy, Hungary, Portugal and Poland.

Members of the Drumglass kindergarten
wear their panama hats in the Dig for
Victory Garden, c.1940

Uniform

When walking to and from our school
Full uniform we don
Or else a prefect's voice is heard
'Please put your beret on!'

H. MCAFEE[20]

School uniform was introduced by Miss Matier and
although the exact date is not now known, it was
seemingly before 1918 and perhaps as early as 1913,
when Victoria College was reconstituted as a public
school. Laura Patterson (née Wood), who joined the
boarding department in 1918, remarked on the thrill
of having a trunk full of new clothes that included a
gymslip and a hat with the school band and badge.
Twenty years later Mary Balfour (née Lindsay) was
equally delighted with her new uniform and recalls
how she stood with pride outside the front door of her
grandmother's house in Broomhill Park, Belfast.[21]

This first uniform comprised a three-pleat
navy-blue gym tunic with a crimson blouse, black
shoes and stockings. A school blazer and a crimson
felt hat akin to 'an inverted pudding basin' were
worn outdoors.[22] The hats bore the school band and

the letters VCB; they were to be worn even if simply
crossing the road to the school tennis courts or going to
and from the University House at 3 Lower Crescent.
The kindergarten children wore a hat or cap with the
letters DHS (Drumglass House School).

In summer, pupils wore a grey one-piece frock
with grey stockings and black shoes. They were also
required to wear a white panama hat, which resembled
'a small umbrella perched on the top of our heads'.
Again, these hats were to be worn at all times when
coming to and going from school, but as Ena Reid (née
Bradford) explains, she and her friends made it their
objective to whip off the offending objects once clear
of the school grounds. On one memorable occasion,
the hatless reprobates were spotted by Miss Brannigan
as she travelled home on the bus. Miss Brannigan,
who taught English and French, duly reported the
girls to the headmistress for bringing the school into
disrepute. They were subsequently given a Saturday
morning detention. This was Ena's only black mark
throughout school, and she has never forgotten it.[23]

Before the formal introduction of school
uniform, there was a dress code of sorts and an
expectation that girls would dress smartly. Mrs Byers
provided guidelines as to what she regarded appropriate
attire and on one occasion fumed about the 'iniquity
of wearing a frill until it was soiled'. The girls wore a
regulation gym suit in their exercise classes, but were
always to wear an ordinary skirt when going to and
from class; modesty was everything.[24]

Post-war changes: The 1940s and 50s

War and the years of rationing inevitably had an
impact on the uniform, which became shabbier. In her
annual report, Mrs Faris declared that patches were
honourable. She also expressed her gratitude that
most parents recognised coupons spent on uniform
were coupons well spent; no doubt this was a gentle
nudge to others who were not of this persuasion.[25]

The year 1948 brought significant changes. The
distinctive maroon tunic was introduced for winter

wear and was worn with a grey blouse, black stockings and black shoes; the younger girls wore knee-length grey stockings. A black beret and navy Burberry or nap coat were worn outdoors. Checked gingham frocks were worn in the summer months. These were in the House colours – red, green, blue or yellow – but the girls were free to wear whichever colour they wished. There was no special hockey outfit at this time and pupils simply wore their school uniform on the sports field and not infrequently travelled home from a match in sodden and muddy gym tunics.[26]

There were additional changes in 1953. Juniors now wore a three-pleat tunic instead of a plain one; the senior uniform comprised a grey skirt and blouse with light grey stockings. It was at this time that the grey Burberry was introduced, worn with a grey beret, and later a maroon one. A new school tie was designed by the art department and incorporated the bee, which both symbolised industry and represented the first letter in Byers. As Miss Cunningham explained:

> It should be a constant reminder that any achievement of ours is made possible by the enterprise and pioneer work of our forbears and that we can only be worthy of our heritage, by, like the honey bee, not the drone, selecting the best from what is offered and making unselfish contributions to the common good.[27]

In 1966 it was decided that fifth and sixth formers should have their own scarf and a design by Katherine Bell was chosen.[28] When the prefect system was replaced by the Sixth-form Council in 1971, the special tie hitherto reserved for prefects was now worn by all members of upper sixth; from 1984 it was worn by all sixth formers.

The amalgamation

Following the amalgamation with Richmond Lodge School in 1987, the uniform was modified to represent this stage in the school's history. A committee headed by Patricia Pyne, head of sixth form, was made responsible for designing the new uniform, which was duly approved by the board of governors. The major change was the introduction of a grey blazer and new ties – a striped blue and maroon tie for juniors; a maroon tie with a blue stripe and the school coat of arms for sixth formers. A maroon skirt was to be worn by all girls in the secondary department, while those in the preparatory department continued to wear the maroon tunic in winter and a striped grey and blue dress in summer. Both the school scarf and the grey V-neck were modified to incorporate a maroon and blue stripe. With the reintroduction of the prefect system in 1997, a new tie was designed for their use. This is maroon with a broad silver band and the school coat of arms.

The winter uniform

SPORT, MUSIC AND ART

I was given a tour of the school and saw evidence of great art, music and sporting talents being nurtured there. [...] South Belfast is fortunate to have so many good schools like Victoria College.
BERNIE KELLY[29]

The number of opportunities available to pupils is ever-expanding. The girls enjoy a variety of sports including golf, cross-country running and creative dance. Rugby, which is now played in the middle school, has proved immensely popular. In 1997 the Northern Ireland Sports Council launched the Sportsmark and awarded this to schools offering a high level of physical recreation, both timetabled and extracurricular. Victoria College was one of twenty-nine schools accorded this honour, a fitting tribute to Ann Morrison in her final year as head of PE. In 1999 Victoria College attained the Goldmark and was one of only six schools in Northern Ireland to be so distinguished.[30] Many pupils have achieved success at national and international level and some have established themselves as British champions.

Music flourishes in the school. The girls perform before family and friends in the school assembly halls and in the homely surroundings of Vita Glass. They compete in competitions and festivals and participate in inter-school events such as the BBC's Making a Difference concert, which was held in the Grand Opera House in March 1999. Thirty members of the senior choir joined participants from other schools and celebrities such as Westlife and Lionel Blair.[31] The school choir has earned an excellent reputation and enjoys opportunities to perform at home and abroad. Notably, in 1995 the choir was invited to give ten concerts throughout America to raise money for the Ulster Project, a charity that enables children from Northern Ireland to holiday in the United States. Each concert was performed in a different state – the tour started in Milwaukee and ended ten days later in Atlanta. In October 1999 the Chamber Choir travelled to Prague to give a series of concerts. The board of governors commissioned Philip Hammond to write a piece of music to mark the occasion, 'Prague Pictures'. A real highlight of the trip was the impromptu performance the girls gave en route and at the request of Mary McAleese, president of Ireland, who happened to be on their flight. The pupils duly regaled passengers and crew with an Irish number.[32] In May 2009 the award-winning junior choir also had an opportunity to perform for President McAleese when she visited Victoria College.

Art at the school remains rich and varied. Pupils visit galleries and exhibitions and are encouraged to explore all aspects of the subject from photography to pottery and fashion design. The girls achieve highly in public examinations and competitions. In 2002 two Victoria pupils were awarded the highest marks in A-level art; a tremendous result and a tribute to the teaching staff. Girls occasionally display their work in galleries and public venues, and each year examination classes hold an open evening for parents, pupils and staff to view and admire their artwork. From 1996 to 1999 much of the school was involved in a cross-curricular project sponsored by the Ulster Bank, the artist-in-residence scheme. In the first year, a local artist worked on an environmental theme with pupils from the preparatory, junior and senior schools; the following years the girls welcomed a theatre designer and a potter, who involved members of staff as well as pupils.

i   Emma Henderson, Ulster and Irish Freestyle and Individual Medley champion for a third consecutive year

ii Sarah Henderson, British Under-19 Speed and Surf Lifesaving Champion, 2008. Sarah was selected for the Great Britain team to compete in the European Championships where she won a bronze medal.

iii Emily Madill who was selected for the Federation Cup Tennis Team, which represented Ireland in the Europe/Africa group held in Malta in April 2009.

iv The chamber choir performing at the BT Woman of the Year awards, 2007

v   In the 2009 Northern Irish team for the London mini marathon, three of the six members were pupils at Victoria: (L–R) Georgia Dick, Rachael Henderson and Ella Davis.

vi The prep relay swimming team, which represented Ireland in the English sixtieth anniversary swimming championships in Sheffield in June 2009: (L–R) Esmee Hall, Eve Wilson, Emma Henderson (captain), Daria Colgan

i   Irish President Mary McAleese visiting Victoria in May 2009: (L–R) Martin McAleese, Mary McAleese, pupil Petra Wells and Ms Slevin

ii Assistant principal Hilary Woods with her husband Leonard Woods at the gala dinner

iii Four past lady wardens with the headmistress at the gala dinner: (L–R) Joanne Brown, Heather Rendell, Ms Slevin, Margaret McVeigh and Helen Robinson

iv Betty Kerr, Elizabeth Bicker and special guest Mary Elise Domvile, great-granddaughter of founder Margaret Byers, at the gala dinner

VICTORIA COLLEGE IN ITS 150TH YEAR

Traditions cannot stand still; if they are not upheld and added to they shrivel away.
GRACE FARIS[33]

In 2009 Victoria College celebrated its 150th anniversary and its distinction as the third oldest girls' school in the United Kingdom. A celebration committee, chaired by Hilary Woods, assistant principal, planned a number of events to commemorate this landmark. The celebrations were launched on 8 January with the raising of a sesquicentennial flag by Lady Carswell OBE, a former pupil. Next came an an open day in January and a magnificent gala dinner in March at the Culloden Hotel, which was attended by four hundred and fifty guests and compèred by the well-known Ulster broadcaster, Wendy Austin, who is also an Old Girl. In May an exhibition of photographs and memorabilia chronicling the school's history was displayed in Drumglass Hall and enjoyed by former pupils and friends, as well as by President McAleese, who asked to visit Victoria in this important year. In June the preparatory department had a Fun Day to celebrate the anniversary and mark the retirement of Joan Cupitt, the much-loved head of the preparatory school. The guest of honour at a special sesquicentennial prize day in September was Nicky Kinnaird, a member of the OGA and founder and president of the highly successful cosmetic retailer, Space NK. A gala concert in the Waterfront Hall in November brought an end to this momentous year.

Victoria College is now the oldest girls' school in Ireland and is proud of its heritage. It builds on strong traditions to uphold and advance its reputation as a progressive institute of learning for girls. With developments in technology, improvements in communication and changing social values, the school today is ostensibly very different to the Victorian establishment that Dr Byers' founded. Yet the ethos has remained constant throughout its long history. Victoria College continues Margaret Byers' ambition to provide girls 'with an education equal to boys' and 'adapted to their wants', and enables pupils to avail themselves of every opportunity to fit them for life and work in an ever-changing world.[34] But most importantly, Victoria College keeps moving, evolving and growing, as its founder intended:

> If Mrs Byers were with us today I think she might say,
> 'I like what you have done now what are you going
> to do next?'[35]
> LADY KEIR

Notes

Chapter 1

1. M. Hull, *The Victorian*, 1959, p. 11.
2. M. Byers, speech to the Endowment's Commission, 1886, reprinted in *The Ladies' Collegiate Magazine*, 1887, p. 5.
3. A. Jordan, *Margaret Byers: Pioneer of Women's Education and Founder of Victoria College, Belfast* (Belfast, The Institute of Irish Studies, 1990), pp. 3–5.
4. M. Byers, speech to the Endowment's Commission, p. 5.
5. E.M. Farrington, *The Victorian*, 1959, p. 17.
6. *The Ladies' Collegiate Report*, 1874–5; M. Byers, 'Victoria College, Belfast, with some account of its connection with the higher education of women in Ireland', VCB archive.
7. A.S. McMordie, VCB archive.
8. E.M. Farrington, *The Victorian*, 1959, p. 16.
9. M. Byers, prize-giving 1902, reprinted in *The Victoria College Magazine*, 1902, p. 61.
10. M. Byers, annual report 1874–5, pp. 7–9, VCB archive; A. Jordan, *Margaret Byers: Pioneer of Women's Education and Founder of Victoria College, Belfast* (Belfast, The Institute of Irish Studies, 1990), pp. 38–9.
11. *The Victoria College Magazine*, 1889, pp. 269–70.
12. L. Patterson, *Laura's a Caution* (Holywood, Priory Press, 1995), pp. 128–9. I am grateful to Mr John Wilson for providing me with excerpts from this, his aunt's, autobiography.
13. M. Byers, 'Victoria College, Belfast', p. 5.
14. A.S. McMordie, VCB archive.
15. M. Byers, prize-giving 1880, reprinted in *The Ladies' Collegiate Report*, 1879–80, p. 21
16. M. Byers, annual report 1900, p. 7, VCB archive.
17. M. Byers, prize-giving 1879, reprinted in *The Ladies' Collegiate Report*, 1878–9, p. 12.
18. A. Jordan, *Margaret Byers*, pp. 27, 29, 86.
19. M. Byers, prize-giving 1880, reprinted in *The Ladies' Collegiate Report*, 1879–80, p. 28; M. Byers, annual report, prize-giving 1894, reprinted in *The Victoria College Magazine*, 1894, p. 52.
20. *The Victoria College Magazine*, 1889, pp. 307–8

21. C. Nesbitt, *A Little Love and Good Company* (London, Faber & Faber, 1975), p. 23.
22. A. Machen, *The Victorian*, 1959, p. 14.
23. A.S. McMordie, *The Victorian*, 1959, p. 10.
24. A. Jordan, *Margaret Byers*, p. 37.
25. Ibid.
26. M. Byers, *The Ladies' Collegiate Magazine*, 1887, p. 109.
27. A. Jordan, *Margaret Byers*.
28. Ibid., p. 18.
29. Ibid., pp. 17–21.
30. M. Byers, annual report 1901, p. 8, VCB archive.
31. M. Byers, prize-giving 1878, reprinted in *The Ladies' Collegiate Report*, 1877–8, p. 16.
32. Newspaper cutting, June 1883, in M. Byers' scrapbook, VCB archive.
33. M. Byers, annual report 1901, pp. 3–4, VCB archive.
34. A. Jordan, paper given to the Old Girls' Assocation (OGA), May 1990, reprinted in *The Victorian*, 1989–90, pp. 130–3 (131).
35. A. Jordan, *Margaret Byers*, p. 16.
36. E.M. Farrington, *The Victorian*, 1959, p. 17.
37. A. Jordan, *Margaret Byers*, p. 16.
38. M. Byers, annual report 1902–3, p. 7, VCB archive.
39. A. Jordan, *Margaret Byers*, p. 16.
40. Ibid., pp. 10–15.
41. Ibid., pp. 15–16.
42. M. Byers, 'Victoria College, Belfast', p. 7.
43. Newspaper cutting, April 1897, in M. Byers' scrapbook, VCB archive; M. Byers, address to the Association of Schoolmasters, Dublin, 1888, reprinted in *The Victoria College Magazine*, 1889, p. 279.
44. M. Byers, prize-giving 1879, reprinted in *The Ladies' Collegiate Report*, 1878–9, pp. 12–13; M. Byers, prize-giving 1877, reprinted in *The Ladies' Collegiate Report*, 1876–7, p. 8; M. Byers, 'Victoria College, Belfast', p. 7.

Chapter 2

1. 'Nora', *from* 'Our College', *The Victoria College Magazine*, 1889, p. 307.
2. M. Byers, address to the Schoolmasters' Association, Dublin 1888, p. 278.
3. *The Victoria College Magazine*, 1887, p. 109.
4. Ibid., p. 76.
5. D.F. Corrigan, *Helen Waddell: A Biography* (London, Victor Gollancz, 1986), p. 50.
6. VCB archive.
7. *The Victorian*, 1959, p. 11; ibid., 1971, pp. 18–19; VCB archive.
8. *The Victorian*, 1959, p. 17; VCB archive.
9. C. Nesbitt, *A Little Love and Good Company*, pp. 23–4.
10. *The Victorian*, 1959, p. 10.
11. A. Jordan, *Margaret Byers*, p. 36; L.N.W., *In Memory of Miss Matier*, supplement to *The Victorian*, 1945, p. 8.
12. *The Victoria College Magazine*, 1890, pp. 522–33; *The Victoria College Magazine*, 1892, pp. 78–9.
13. *The Victoria College Magazine*, 1890, p. 511.
14. The *Victoria College Magazine*, 1889, pp. 375–82; N. Robb, *A History of Richmond Lodge School* (Belfast, n.p., c.1967), p. 10.
15. A. Jordan, *Margaret Byers*, p. 26.
16. Ibid., pp. 28–9; M. Byers, handwritten addendum to annual report 1900, VCB archive.
17. M. Byers, annual report 1901, pp. 9–10, VCB archive.
18. A. Jordan, *Margaret Byers*, pp. 37–8.
19. Ibid., p. 29.
20. B. Grimshaw, *The Blue Book Magazine*, April 1939, http://pulprack.com/arch/2003/02/beatrice_grimsh.html
21. C. Connor, *The Victoria College Magazine*, 1889, p. 327.
22. Copies of these letters are held in the VCB archive.
23. M. Byers, 'Victoria College, Belfast'.
24. M. Byers, address to the Association of Schoolmasters, Dublin, 1888, p. 281.
25. A.S. McMordie, *The Victorian*, 1959, p. 10.
26. A. Jordan, *Margaret Byers*, p. 54; *The Victoria College Magazine*, 1888, p. 175; *The Victoria College Magazine*, 1889, p. 327.
27. C. Nesbitt, *A Little Love and Good Company*, p. 23.
28. A. Matier, on the occasion of the unveiling of a portrait of the head mistress, VCB archive.
29. *The Victoria College Magazine*, 1931, pp. 41–2.
30. A. Jordan, *Margaret Byers*, pp. 58–60.
31. *The Victoria College Magazine*, 1890, pp. 556–7.
32. A. Jordan, *Margaret Byers*, pp. 60–2.

33 I. Woods, *Wheels of Change: An Autobiography* (Belfast, Shanway Press, 2008), pp. 8–9.

34 M. Byers, response to presentation made by staff and pupils, 1905, VCB archive.

35 *The Victoria College Magazine*, 1890, pp. 510–12.

36 M. Byers, response to presentation; The Victoria Homes Trust, www.victoriahomestrust.org.uk/2.html

37 *The Victoria College Magazine*, 1887, p. 76.

38 L.C. Purser, 6 July 1905, quoted in *Victoria College Belfast Centenary 1859–1959* (Belfast, n.p., c.1959), p. 14.

39 L.C. Purser, *News Letter*, 22 February 1912.

40 M. Hull, *The Victorian*, 1959, p. 11.

41 *The Victorian*, 1956, pp. 19–20.

42 L.C. Purser, 6 July 1905, quoted in *Victoria College Belfast Centenary 1859–1959*, pp. 13–14.

43 Ibid.

44 M. Byers, prize-giving 1903, p. 8, VCB archive.

45 W.B. Yeats, quoted by M. Finch, *The Victorian*, 1979, p. 18.

46 A. Jordan, *Margaret Byers*, pp. 33–4.

47 1889 prospectus, reprinted in A. Jordan, *Margaret Byers*, pp. 77–92 (86); *The Victorian*, 1980, p. 18.

48 M. Hull, *The Victorian*, 1959, p. 12.

49 A.S. McMordie, VCB archive; M. Hull, *The Victorian*, 1959, pp. 11–13.

50 M. Hull, *The Victorian*, 1959, pp. 11–12.

51 E.M. Farrington, *The Victorian*, 1972, pp. 24–5.

52 A. Jordan, *Margaret Byers*, pp. 37, 29–30.

53 M. Hull, *The Victorian*, 1959, p. 12.

54 E.M. Farrington, *The Victorian*, 1959, p. 17.

55 L. Patterson, *Laura's a Caution*, pp. 126–9; 136–8.

56 M. Hull, *The Victorian*, 1959, p. 12.

57 Annual report of upper-sixth boarders paraphrasing Oliver Goldsmith, *The Victorian*, 1983, p. 58.

58 K. Davey, VCB archive.

59 M. Balfour, VCB archive.

60 R. Carswell, *The Victorian*, 1992–3, p. 33.

61 Ibid., pp. 32–3; K. Faris, ibid., 1969, pp. 19–21; A. Morrison and A. Maddocks, VCB archive.

62 A. Maddocks, VCB archive.

63 E. Hunter, VCB archive.

64 A. Morrison, VCB archive.

65 *The Victorian*, 1986, p. 24.

66 Ibid.

67 C. Young, VCB archive.

68 Ibid.

69 *The Victorian*, 1985, pp. 57–8.

70 Ibid., 1977, p. 51; ibid., 1980, p. 77; B. Berner, personal correspondence, 2009.

Chapter 3

1 H. Pollock, address to Miss Matier upon her retirement, *The Witness*, 9 January 1931.

2 Handwritten memorandum, 23 May 1912, VCB archive.

3 *The Victorian*, 1950, p. 23.

4 S. Acheson, *In Memory of Miss Matier*, supplement to *The Victorian*, 1945, pp. 8–9.

5 Advertisement for school, newspaper cutting, September 1913, VCB archive.

6 A. Matier, annual reports 1914 and 1924, VCB archive.

7 H. Waddell, *The Witness*, 9 January 1931.

8 S. Acheson, *In Memory of Miss Matier*, p. 8.

9 A. Machen, *The Victorian*, 1959, p. 14; H. Waddell, *In Memory of Miss Matier*, p. 3.

10 A. Matier, annual report 1914, VCB archive.

11 E.K.L., *In Memory of Miss Matier*, pp. 11–12; E.M.F., *The Victorian*, 1931, p. 3.

12 K. Davey, VCB archive.

13 H. Waddell, *The Witness*, 9 January 1931.

14 S. Campbell Smith, *In Memory of Miss Matier*, p. 14.

15 L.N.W., *In Memory of Miss Matier*, p. 8.

16 Ibid., p. 7; E. Bishop, *The Victorian*, 1947, pp. 28–9.

17 M. Rogers, *The Victorian*, 1959, p. 19.

18 S. Finnegan, *The Witness*, 9 January 1931.

19 G. Faris, *The Witness*, 9 January, 1931.

20 J. Baxter and E.K.L., *In Memory of Miss Matier*, pp. 12, 16; *The Victorian*, 1945, p. 27.

21 Quoted in D.F. Corrigan, *Helen Waddell*, p. 79.

22 A. Matier, annual report 1918, VCB archive; K. Davey, VCB archive.

23 J. Baxter and S. Campbell Smith, *In Memory of Miss Matier*,, pp. 14, 16.

24 S. Acheson, *The Victorian*, 1931, pp. 17–18; Mary Rogers, *The Victorian*, 1959, p. 19.

25 *The Victorian*, 1944, pp. 29–30; ibid., 1945, p. 22.

26 E. Bishop, *The Victorian*, 1947, pp. 28–9.

27 A. Matier, annual report 1917, VCB archive.

28 Ibid.

29 *Northern Whig*, 16 September 1916.

30 *Northern Whig*, 23 December 1914.

31 A. Matier, annual report 1917, VCB archive.

32 R. McLernon, *The Victorian*, 1960, p. 40.

33 A. Matier, annual report 1920, VCB archive.

34 H.M. Pollock, *In Memory of Miss Matier*, p. 6.

35 A. Matier, annual report 1924, VCB archive.

36 E.K.L., *In Memory of Miss Matier*, p. 12; *The Victorian*, 1945, p. 27.

37 School prospectus, VCB archive.

38 A. Jordan, *Margaret Byers*, pp. 25–6, 30–1.

39 *The Witness*, 9 January 1931.

40 A. Matier, annual report 1922, VCB archive.

41 M. Rogers, *The Victorian*, 1959, p. 19; L.N.W., *In Memory of Miss Matier*, p. 6.

42 A. Matier, annual report 1922, VCB archive.

43 VCB board minutes, PRONI SCH/653/3; W. Cunningham, *Belfast Telegraph*, 13 February 1974.

44 VCB archive.

45 A. Matier, annual report, *Belfast Telegraph*, 27 June 1924.

46 *Victoria College Belfast Centenary 1859–1959*, p. 34.

47 VCB board minutes, PRONI SCH/653/3.

48 B. Berner, VCB archive

49 Ibid.

50 Ibid.

51 VCB archive.

52 *Victoria College Belfast Centenary 1859–1959*, pp. 32–4; www.strathearn.org.uk

53 A. Matier, presentation to mark her retirement, *The Witness*, 3 January 1931.

54 Quoted in D.F. Corrigan, *Helen Waddell*, p. 208.

55 K. Davey, VCB archive.

56 L.N.W., *In Memory of Miss Matier*, p. 8.

Chapter 4

1 R. McLernon, unveiling of Mrs Faris' portrait, 28 February 1952, *The Victorian*, 1952, p. 14.

[2] J.H. Withers, *The Victorian*, 1974, p. 21.

[3] *Victoria College Belfast Centenary 1859–1959*, p. 20.

[4] *The Victorian*, 1943, pp. 23–4.

[5] A. Graham, *The Victorian*, 1972, p. 26.

[6] VCB archive.

[7] G. Faris, *The Victorian*, 1937, pp. 9–10; ibid., 1938, p. 29.

[8] Ibid., 1940, p. 19.

[9] J. Ardill, VCB archive.

[10] G. Faris, prize-giving 1939, reprinted in *The Victorian*, 1940, p. 18.

[11] *The Victorian*, 1943, p. 17.

[12] VCB archive.

[13] G. Faris, *The Victorian*, 1946, p. 21.

[14] M. Balfour, VCB archive.

[15] VCB board minutes, March 1941, PRONI SCH/653/3; G. Faris, prize-giving 1941, reprinted in *The Victorian*, 1942, p. 16.

[16] *The Victorian*, 1970, pp. 14–15, 20; A. Cumming, VCB archive.

[17] VCB Board Minutes, March 1941, PRONI; Mrs Faris, prize-giving 1941, *The Victorian*, 1942, p. 16; Robb, *History of Richmond Lodge*, pp. 48–9; A. Cumming and R. Carswell, VCB archive.

[18] A. Wasson, annual report, *The Victorian*, 1943, p. 20.

[19] R. Carswell, VCB archive.

[20] Ibid.

[21] VCB archive; *The Victorian*, 1980, p. 22; ibid., 1974, p. 27.

[22] *The Victorian*, 1942, p. 18.

[23] A. Cumming, VCB archive.

[24] VCB archive.

[25] R. Carswell and A. Maddocks, VCB archive

[26] *The Victorian*, 1946, pp. 19, 22; R. Carswell, VCB archive.

[27] G. Faris, *The Victorian*, 1942, p.13.

[28] *The Victorian* 1959, pp. 21–2; VCB archive.

[29] *The Victorian*, 1943, p. 31; ibid., 1945, p. 44; ibid., 1941, p. 15.

[30] M. McKelvey, M. Balfour, VCB archive.

[31] *The Victorian*, 1959, p. 22.

[32] Ibid., 1943, p. 17.

[33] Ibid., 1944, p. 25.

[34] VCB archive.

[35] B. Berner, VCB archive.

[36] M. McKelvey, J. Moran, VCB archive; *The Victorian*, 1970, p. 20.

[37] *The Victorian*, Ibid., 1942, p. 16.

[38] G. Faris, ibid., 1946, p. 21.

[39] Ibid., p. 22; M.L., ibid., 1974, p. 26.

[40] W. Cunningham, prize-giving 1951, reprinted in *The Victorian*, 1952,

pp. 25–6.

[41] *The Victorian*, 1950, p. 41.

[42] G. Faris, ibid., 1938, p. 17.

[43] *The Victorian*, 1952, p. 15.

[44] F. Allen, VCB archive.

[45] VCB archive.

[46] M.G. McN, *The Victorian*, 1953, pp. 21–2.

[47] VCB archive; M.G. McN, *The Victorian*, 1953, pp. 21–2; J.E.K, ibid., 1966, p. 17.

[48] J. Moran, VCB archive.

[49] B. Kerr, VCB archive.

[50] VCB archive.

[51] Ibid.

[52] R. McLernon, *The Victorian*, 1964, pp. 18–19.

[53] B. Berner, VCB archive; E. Elder, *The Victorian*, 1962, pp. 21–2; A. Maddocks and B. Kerr, VCB archive. Jeannie Hall was the colleague encountered in Innsbruck.

[54] R.M.H, *The Victorian*, 1967, p. 20.

[55] *The Victorian*, 1960, p. 27.

[56] W. Cunningham, prize-giving 1967, reprinted in *The Victorian*, 1968, pp. 13–14.

[57] S. Lyons, *The Victorian*, 1963, p. 28.

[58] W. Cunningham, prize-giving 1967, reprinted in *The Victorian*, 1968, pp. 13–14.

[59] G. Faris, *The Victorian*, 1945, p. 22.

[60] Ibid.

[61] Ibid., 1949, p. 18; ibid., 1950, p. 20.

[62] Report of board of governors, prize-giving 1950, reprinted in *The Victorian*, 1951, pp. 20–1.

[63] M. Moore, registrar of Victoria College, on the occasion of Mrs Faris' retirement, *The Victorian*, 1952, p. 15.

[64] G. Faris, *The Victorian* 1940, p. 16.

[65] E.A.G., *The Victorian*, 1974, p. 25.

[66] *The Victorian*, 1952, p. 18.

[67] VCB board minutes, PRONI SCH/653/3.

[68] I am indebted to Patricia Pyne for her generous help and advice. This section draws extensively on her account of the armorial bearings in *The Victorian*, 1987–8, pp. 19–20, as well as A.S. McMordie, VCB archive, and W. Cunningham, annual report, prize-giving 1953, reprinted in *The Victorian*, 1954, p. 16.

Chapter 5

[1] W. Cunningham, *The Victorian*, 1961, p. 15.

[2] Lady Carswell, *Memories of a Headmistress: Weir Cunningham* (Belfast,

OGA, *c*.2004), VCB archive.

[3] *Belfast Telegraph*, 13 February 1974.

[4] *News Letter*, 12 October 1959.

[5] *The Victorian*, 1968, p. 45; ibid., 1972, pp. 13–14.

[6] W. Cunningham, interview with the *Belfast Telegraph*, 13 February 1974.

[7] VCB archive; *The Victorian*, 1958, p. 42.

[8] S. Faulkner, personal correspondence 2009; *The Victorian*, 1977, p. 44.

[9] N. Watts, *The Victorian*, 1977, p. 40.

[10] W. Cunningham, prize-giving 1955, reprinted in *The Victorian*, 1956, p. 15.

[11] M. Lamb, N. McCavana and S. Murray, *The Victorian*, 1972, pp. 26–30.

[12] VCB archive.

[13] J. Hall, VCB archive; W. Cunningham, prize-giving 1953, reprinted in *The Victorian*, 1954, p. 12.

[14] N. McCavana, *The Victorian*, 1972, p. 28.

[15] School prospectus, 1960s, VCB archive.

[16] D. Walsh, *Memories of a Headmistress*, VCB archive.

[17] *The Victorian*, 1969, p. 12.

[18] Ibid., 1967, p. 61.

[19] Ibid., 1971, p. 39.

[20] A. Morrison, VCB archive; *News Letter*, 15 March 1972; *The Victorian*, 1972, p. 42.

[21] *The Victorian*, 1977, pp. 21–3.

[22] Winston Churchill, quoted by pupils who enjoyed a trip to Switzerland in 1963, *The Victorian*, 1964, p. 40.

[23] P. Pyne, personal correspondence, 2009.

[24] *The Victorian*, 1989–90, pp. 35–6; ibid, 1991–2, p. 46.

[25] VCB archive.

[26] W. Cunningham, quoted in the *Belfast Telegraph*, 13 February 1974.

[27] A. Kirkpatrick, personal correspondence, 2009.

[28] M.J.R., *The Victorian*, 1998–9, p. 17; W. Cunningham, ibid., 1971, p. 15; ibid., p. 21.

[29] A. Graham, *The Victorian*, 1985, pp. 47–50; B. Kerr, VCB archive.

[30] N. McCavana, *The Victorian*, 1972, p. 28.

[31] A. Morrison, VCB archive.

[32] Miss Elizabeth Lindsay, 'the former colleague', would recount this tale with great delight.

[33] *The Victorian*, 1989–90, p. 128.

[34] E.M. Farrington, *The Victorian*, 1960, p. 14.

35 Ibid., p. 13.

36 *Victoria College Belfast Centenary 1858–1959* (Belfast, n.p., *c.*1959).

37 *The Victorian*, 1987, p. 14.

38 G. Faris, *The Victorian*, 1959.

39 Ibid., 1957, pp. 19–20.

40 W. Cunningham, prize-giving 1955, reprinted in *The Victorian*, 1956, p. 16.

41 Ibid., p. 15; ibid., 1964, p. 12.

42 W. Cunningham, prize-giving 1962, reprinted in *The Victorian*, 1963, pp. 13–14.

43 W. Cunningham, prize-giving 1963, reprinted in *The Victorian*, 1964, pp. 12–13; W. Cunningham, prize-giving 1964, reprinted in *The Victorian*, 1965, p. 13.

44 W. Cunningham, prize-giving 1963, reprinted in *The Victorian*, 1964, pp. 12–13; Cunningham, prize-giving 1977, *The Victorian*, 1978, p. 15.

45 K. Faris, *The Victorian*, 1961, p. 10.

46 W. Cunningham, prize-giving, 1955, reprinted in *The Victorian*, 1956, p. 15.

47 *The Victorian*, 1961, p. 13; ibid., 1962, p. 15.

48 N. Watts, *The Victorian*, 1966, p. 10.

49 J.H. Withers, *The Victorian*, 1969, p. 17.

50 S. Murray, *The Victorian*, 1972, p. 30

51 *Belfast Telegraph*, 13 February 1974.

52 *The Victorian*, 1973, p. 11.

53 *The Victorian*, 1973, p. 23.

54 W. Cunningham, prize-giving 1972, reprinted in *The Victorian*, 1973, p.25.

55 M. Gibson, from 'The new Victoria', *The Victorian*, 1972, p. 11.

56 VCB archive; J. Ardill, personal correspondence, 2009.

57 *The Victorian*, 1973, pp. 13, 37–8.

58 www.crescentarts.org

59 *Belfast Telegraph*, October 1975, VCB archive.

60 *The Victorian*, 1975, pp. 13, 16.

61 M.J.R., *The Victorian*, 1970, p. 9.

62 *The Victorian*, 1972, pp. 58, 61; ibid., 1974, p. 43.

63 *The Victorian*, 1972, pp. 13–14.

64 W. Cunningham, *The Victorian*, 1976, p. 15.

65 M.J.R., *The Victorian*, 1977, p. 45.

66 B. Kerr, *Memories of a Headmistress*, VCB archive.

67 VCB archive.

68 *The Ladies' Collegiate Magazine*, 1886, p. 50.

69 *The Victoria College Magazine*, 1888, p. 175.

70 Ibid., 1887, p. 109.

71 R. McLernon, *The Victorian*, 1946, p. 19.

72 M. Byers, annual report 1901, p. 10, VCB archive; ibid., 1902–3, p. 1.

73 E.M. Farrington, *The Victorian Jubilee Edition 1915–65*, 1965, p. 26.

74 *The Victorian*, 1946, p. 19.

Chapter 6

1 *The Victorian*, 1987, p. 8.

2 B. Berner, *The Victorian*, 1987–8, p. 16.

3 B. Berner, VCB archive.

4 B. Berner, *The Victorian*, 1978, p. 13.

5 *The Victorian*, 1978, pp. 13–14; ibid., 1979, pp. 13–14; ibid., 1980, p. 15.

6 B. Berner, prize-giving 1977, reprinted in *The Victorian*, 1978, pp. 13–14.

7 *The Victorian*, 1981, p. 16; ibid., 1986, p. 13.

8 B. Berner, *The Victorian*, 1978, p. 14.

9 *The Victorian*, 1994–5, p. 26.

10 B. Berner, prize-giving 1986, reprinted in *The Victorian*, 1987, p. 9.

11 J. Higginson, *The Victorian*, 1991–2, p. 22.

12 *The Victorian*, 1978, p. 64; ibid., 1990–1, p. 39.

13 Ibid, 1997–8, pp. 6, 68.

14 J. Boyle, VCB archive.

15 Ibid.

16 A. Morrison, VCB archive.

17 B. Berner, *The Victorian*, 1987, p. 9.

18 J. Russell, *The Victorian*, 1987, p. 16.

19 Ibid.

20 *The Victorian*, 1988–9, p. 13.

21 Ibid., 1987–8, p. 25.

22 D. McCullough, *The Victorian*, 2005–6, p. 18.

23 N. Hall, personal correspondence, 2009.

24 P. Pyne, VCB archive.

25 J. Higginson, *The Victorian*, 1990–1, p. 16.

26 M. Andrews, *The Victorian*, 1992–3, p. 13.

27 *The Victorian*, 1989–90, pp. 17–19.

28 Ibid., 1991–2, p. 13.

29 Ibid., pp. 29–33.

30 A. McBride and P. Pyne, *The Victorian*, 1992–3, p. 30.

31 Ibid., p. 30

32 M. Andrews, *The Victorian*, 1992–3, p. 12.

33 This account draws extensively on N. Robb, *A History of Richmond Lodge School*.

34 N. Robb, *Richmond Lodge*, p. 7.

35 Ibid., p. 8.

36 Ibid., p. 19.

37 Ibid., pp. 75–6.

38 Ibid., p. 37.

39 Ibid., p. 53.

40 *The Victorian*, 1949, pp. 45–6.

41 Ibid., 2000–1, pp. 7–8.

42 J. Cupitt, personal correspondence, 2009.

Chapter 7

1 J. Russell, *The Victorian*, 1999–2000, p. 4.

2 P. Slevin, *The Victorian*, 2004–5, p. 15.

3 M. Andrews, personal correspondence, 2009.

4 N. Hall, personal correspondence, 2009.

5 M. Carwile, from 'A tribute to Mrs Andrews', *The Victorian*, 2004–5, p. 55.

6 B. Kerr, personal correspondence, 2009.

7 P. Slevin, interview in *The Victorian*, 2005–6, p. 16.

8 H. Woods, personal correspondence, 2009.

9 H. Lyons, personal correspondence, 2009.

10 K. Kerr, personal correspondence, 2009.

11 D. Barr, *The Victorian*, 2005–6, p. 7.

12 M. Andrews, *The Victorian*, 2000–1, p. 4.

13 H. Lyons, 2009.

14 *The Victorian*, 1999–2000, pp. 19–20.

15 M. Andrews, *The Victorian*, 2003–4, p. 4.

16 Ibid., 1999–2000, p. 5.

17 *The Victorian*, 2006–7, p. 9.

18 Ibid., 2001–2, pp. 16–17; ibid., 2000–1, p. 8.

19 E. Armstrong, *The Victorian*, 1999–2000, pp. 18–19.

20 H. McAfee, from 'School Punishments', *The Victorian*, 1957, p. 31.

21 L. Patterson, *Laura's a Caution*, p. 126; VCB archive.

22 E. Bishop, *The Victorian*, 1947, p. 29.

23 E. Reid, VCB archive.

24 A.S. McMordie, VCB archive.

25 *The Victorian*, 1944, p. 27.

26 VCB archive.

27 *The Victorian*, 1954, p. 16.

28 W. Cunningham, annual report, prize-giving 1966, reprinted in *The Victorian*, 1967, pp. 11–12.

29 B. Kelly, deputy mayor of Belfast, *South Belfast News*, 14 May 2008.

30 *The Victorian*, 1996–7, p. 5; ibid., 1999–2000, p. 10.

31 Ibid., 1998–9, p. 37.

32 Ibid., 1994–5, p. 45; ibid., 1999–2000, pp. 31–2.

33 G. Faris, *The Victorian*, 1955, p. 17.

34 M. Byers, speech to the Endowment's Commission, *The Ladies Collegiate Magazine*, 1887, p. 5.

35 Lady Keir, *The Victorian*, 1960, p. 39.

Sources

Corrigan, Dame Felicitas, *Helen Waddell: A Biography* (London: Victor Gollancz, 1986)

Jordan, Alison, *Margaret Byers: Pioneer of Women's Education and Founder of Victoria College, Belfast* (Belfast: Institute of Irish Studies, Queen's University Belfast, 1990)

Moore, Mary E., Sadie I. Turkington, Norah L. Watts and Kathleen White, *Victoria College Belfast Centenary 1859–1959* (Belfast,1959)

Nesbitt, Cathleen, *A Little Love and Good Company* (London: Faber & Faber, 1975)

Public Record Office of Northern Ireland, *Ministry/Department of Education Archive (Nov. 2007)*, http://www.proni.gov.uk/introduction__education_archive-2.pdf

Robb, Nesca, *A History of Richmond Lodge School* (Belfast, *c.*1967)

School magazines: *The Ladies' Collegiate Magazine* (1886–7), *The Victoria College Magazine* (1887–1906); *The Victorian* (1916–present)

Victoria College Belfast archive, held at Victoria College

Victoria College Belfast website: http://www.victoriacollege.org.uk/

Woods, Isabel, *Wheels of Change* (Belfast: Shanway Press, 2008)

Chairmen of the board

The board of governors has its origins in 1912 when a small company was formed to take ownership of the school which duly became a public institution. The company was headed by the Rt Hon. Hugh Macdowell Pollock. In 1922 Victoria College entered into an agreement with the new Ministry of Education (NI) and a fully-fledged board of governors was established.

Rt Hon Hugh Macdowell Pollock, PC, MP, DL	1922–37
J. Milne Barbour (Sir Milne Barbour, baronet), DL, MP	1937–46
Rev. John Waddell (The Very Rev. Dr Waddell), DD	1946–9
Professor Gilbert Waterhouse MA, Litt. D., MRIA	1949–50
Mrs Lydia Watts, MB	1950–1
Professor Gilbert Waterhouse MA, Litt. D., MRIA	1951–7
Mrs Elizabeth McCaughey	1957–62
Mrs Lydia Norah Watts, MB	1962–72
Mrs Margaret S. Maginess, ATCL	1973–6
Professor John Acheson Faris, BLitt, MA	1976–85
Mrs Margaret Joan Russell, BA	1985–90
Mr John Willoughby Wilson, QC, MA, LLB	1990–5
Prof. David Robert Hadden, MD, FRCP	1995–2002
Mr Christopher G. Maccabe, LLB, LLM	2002–9
Dr B. J. Gregory, BSc, PhD	2009–

Index

Page numbers in italics refer to pages with photographs.

All of you new girls and those of you who have been Victorians for many years […]
have the privilege of belonging to this old and great school, a school to which
thousands of women all over the world look back with affection and gratitude for
the encouragement, help and opportunities which they received during their
education here. You are the heirs to its traditions and we Old Victorians look to you
to uphold the traditions and good name of the school. Traditions cannot stand still;
if they are not upheld and added to they shrivel away.

GRACE FARIS, *THE VICTORIAN*, 1955, P. 17